W9-ATN-893

March
2018

... For Matt Creighton ...

... Friend of George
Ireland, Coach

... Fan of Loyola
Ramblers Team

1963 Through 2018
and beyond

RAMBLE ON!

LOYOLA'S UNFORGETTABLE 2018 TOURNAMENT RUN

Chicago Tribune

R. Bruce Dold, Publisher & Editor-in-Chief
Peter Kendall, Managing Editor
Christine W. Taylor, Managing Editor
Amy Carr, Associate Managing Editor/Features
Robin Daughtridge, Associate Managing Editor/Photography
Joe Knowles, Associate Managing Editor/Sports
Tim Bannon, Sports Editor

RAMBLE ON!

Copyright © 2018 by *Chicago Tribune*

No part of this publication may be reproduced, stored in a retrieval system, or transmitted in any form by any means, electronic, mechanical, photocopying, or otherwise, without prior written permission of the publisher, Triumph Books LLC, 814 North Franklin Street; Chicago, Illinois 60610.

This book is book is available in quantity at special discounts for your group or organization. For further information, contact:

Triumph Books LLC
814 North Franklin Street
Chicago, Illinois 60610
Phone: (312) 337-0747
www.triumphbooks.com

Printed in U.S.A.
ISBN: 978-1-62937-554-0

Content packaged by Mojo Media, Inc.
Joe Funk: Editor
Jason Hinman: Creative Director

Front and back cover by
John J. Kim/Chicago Tribune

This is an unofficial publication. This book is in no way affiliated with, licensed by or endorsed by the NCAA or Loyola University Chicago.

John J. Kim/Chicago Tribune

CONTENTS

INTRODUCTION

By Chicago Tribune Editorial Board

Some teams swagger into the NCAA basketball tournament with the air of royalty. Then there are teams like the Loyola Ramblers, who surprise with their prowess and poise.

The dream of another national title has faded on Sheridan Road. Sure, it hurts.

But Loyola fans, take heart. This was a brilliant 32-6 Ramblers season that defied odds, predictions and office pools. A championship run that appealed not just to Chicagoans but also to anyone who roots for the Davids of the world against the Goliaths.

Chicagoans often measure time not just in days and weeks, but also the years – sometimes decades – between championship teams. In college basketball, Chicago's drought started in 1963, after the Ramblers won a national title in overtime against Cincinnati.

That just underscores the unfortunate truth: This isn't a college basketball Titletown. Or even a basketball Titlestate. Which makes this magical season even more extraordinary.

The teams with confidence, the been-here-won-that bravado, may believe that history is destiny, that the big squash the small.

But this year the Also Rans include many of the biggest brand names in college basketball. UCLA, with its packed trophy case from its Wizard of Westwood years, didn't travel to San Antonio. Nor did powerhouse University of North Carolina, Michael Jordan's alma mater. Or fabled Kentucky, with more Division I basketball victories than any other school. Traditional powers near the top of that list, such as Duke and Syracuse, also glumly sit on the sidelines.

This year the team that made history is a small, academically excellent Jesuit school on Lake Michigan.

A team shoved into Chicago's basketball shadows by another, bigger Catholic university, DePaul, and its era of the Coaches Meyer, Ray and son Joey.

A team with a 98-year-old nun as its chaplain/mascot whose trademark phrase is "Worship, work and win." Anyone else hear the echoes of the famous "Friday Night Lights" football mantra: "Clear Eyes, Full Hearts, Can't Lose."

Despite this stinging loss, Loyola, the school and the basketball program, is launched on a new trajectory. Loyola is no longer a Chicago sports trivia question. Its success this season will draw students – and, we expect, top basketball recruits.

Near the end of the tournament, coach Porter Moser recalled the days of empty bleachers, "when I could hit a golf ball in that arena (Joseph J. Gentile Arena) ... and hit the stands." He vowed that the team, the school, wouldn't go back to those days. We believe him. This team earned fans' devotion with its grit, hustle and heart.

Think of the great, and near-great teams in Chicago history. The Bulls, Bears, Sox, Cubs, Blackhawks in the years when they almost won it all. The teams that played hard and fell short. The 2018 Loyola Ramblers now take their place among teams that Chicagoans honor not because they reached the pinnacle, but because they soared beyond anyone's reckoning or expectation.

Thanks, Ramblers, for a season that thrilled Chicago. ■

The Loyola Ramblers student section cheers as their team takes the court in San Antonio. (Brian Cassella/Chicago Tribune)

Loyola players arrive for their Final Four semifinal game against the Michigan Wolverines, the culmination of an unbelievable 2018 journey. (John J. Kim/ Chicago Tribune)

BRAVO, LOYOLA

A Story for the Ages

BY STEVE ROSENBLOOM

The feisty and fundamentally solid Loyola Ramblers were never ranked.

The disrespected Ramblers would've missed the NCAA tournament had they not won the Missouri Valley Conference tournament.

The revelation that became the Ramblers nearly played for the national title.

From largely unknown to nearly unbeatable.

Sounds like a movie, and you could do worse than cast Armie Hammer as coach Porter Moser and Helen Mirren as Sister Jean.

But no. Wait. This was better. This was real life. The Ramblers reached the Final Four.

But no. Wait. This was worse. This was real life. The Ramblers ended their season in the Final Four.

Bravo and bitterness. Bravo for the courage to grab greatness. Bitterness in falling short of writing arguably the greatest story in college basketball history.

The gash of the second-half blitzkrieg executed by Michigan on Saturday likely still is bleeding out. Apply some pressure to the wound the way the third-seeded Wolverines applied pressure at Loyola's end of the court and appreciate the gift of the way the 11th-seeded Ramblers ran into sports' heart.

Loyola Ramblers head coach Porter Moser steps through the center court logo during practice at the Alamodome. Moser's trust and belief in his players never wavered during their Cinderella run. (John J. Kim/Chicago Tribune)

They played a beautiful game. The kind of game people fell in love with.

On some teams, star-driven teams, it's obvious which player will take the last shot. On the Ramblers, it was not. On the Ramblers, it was the guy who had the ball, and everybody else was OK with that because everybody else had faith in their teammates.

See Donte Ingram against Miami in the first round for details.

Or Clayton Custer against Tennessee in the next game.

Or Marques Townes against Nevada in the Sweet Sixteen.

Against Kansas State in the Elite Eight, there was no need for a hero shot because Ben Richardson was a hero all game, strafing the Wildcats with three-pointers while scoring a career-high 23 points.

In the national semifinal against Michigan, Cinderella's glass Nikes cracked against a bigger, better team.

It was going to take a better team to beat the kind of team ball Loyola played. No, not played - excelled at. It was all about team. What other programs yammer on about, Loyola lived.

They played a beautiful game. The kind of game people fell in love with. They moved the ball. They continued to move the ball. They moved the ball again. A good shot isn't a great shot, and they selflessly insisted on finding the teammate who was open for the great shot.

That speaks to great coaching and smart players willing to buy in. That also speaks to zero ego on the roster. There was no "my turn" basketball here.

There was no "my turn" spotlight, either. Criticism surfaced regarding the coverage of Sister Jean, the 98-year-old nun and team chaplain. Focus on the players, some critics said. It's not fair to the guys doing the sweating and winning, critics said. They were the ones who deserved it.

But, as expected, the players were fine with whatever coverage came their way and whatever coverage showered Sister Jean. Players seemed to get a kick out of the storyline, the residue of their respect for the person, her beliefs and the tenets of the program.

Such maturity. Such poise. Such a great story - nearly one of the greatest underdog tales every written.

And it's a Chicago school, of all things. In a city that shows little passion for college sports, the Ramblers stoked the romance in a big way. Group hug, everybody.

This probably reads like one of those "participation trophy" pieces, but it shouldn't. Reaching the Final Four is a big deal, especially for a school with little to brag about for three decades.

Again, it sounds like a script, and it still might turn into one. But for now it's real life.

It's why sports is the best reality show – check that, the only reality show. You never know whether it'll be the best or the worst, but it'll be life its own self, true and honest.

Bravo, Loyola, for a special season. ∎

No longer strangers to the national spotlight, the Loyola Ramblers practice at the Alamodome ahead of their Final Four contest against Michigan. (John J. Kim/Chicago Tribune)

John J. Kim/Chicago Tribune

ONWARD AND UPWARD

Top 10 Moments from Loyola's 2018 NCAA Tournament Run

By Shannon Ryan

1. Ingram's Buzzer-Beater

Donte Ingram's buzzer-beating 3-pointer to beat No. 6 seed Miami 64-62 in the first round of the NCAA tournament was a sign of the wild ride that was to come for Loyola. The Ramblers immediately became the talk of the tournament as they raced around the court in Dallas and celebrated in front of their loyal fans. Ingram, a senior, took a pass from Marques Townes and drained it with 0.3 seconds left on the clock.

2. Sister Jean

Loyola's team chaplain Sister Jean Dolores Schmidt became an "international celebrity" and said she had the time of her life at the tournament. That's saying something considering she is 98 years old. The lasting image of Sister Jean: Sitting in her wheelchair in the corner of the court after each victory receiving celebratory hugs from players. She traveled with the Ramblers from St. Louis at the Missouri Valley Conference tournament to stops in Dallas, Atlanta and San Antonio for the NCAA tournament, and the nation learned why Loyola players adore her.

Brian Cassella/Chicago Tribune

John J. Kim/Chicago Tribune

3. Custer's Bounce

Following up on Ingram's buzzer-beater, Clayton Custer hit a shot just about as dramatic to beat No. 3 seed Tennessee 63-62 in a second-round victory. The point guard knocked in a jumper with 3.6 seconds remaining, watching from his back on the court as the ball bounced off the rim, up to the top of the backboard and somehow rattled through the net. It was another big shot that proved the Ramblers were a fun team to watch through the tournament.

4. Townes' Turn

In a 69-68 Sweet 16 victory against No. 7 Nevada in Atlanta, Marques Townes hit a crucial 3-pointer with 6.2 seconds left on the clock. Clayton Custer drove and kicked it out to Townes in the corner. The New Jersey native finished with 18 points.

5. Richardson's Night

Ben Richardson was the Missouri Valley Conference defensive player of the year and is known more for his ability to lock down an opponent rather than to score. His best friend and teammate Clayton Custer said he told Richardson to shoot more. Against No. 9 seed Kansas State, Richardson scored a career-high 23 points in a surprisingly decisive 78-62 victory as the Ramblers earned a trip to the Final Four.

6. Campus Central

Loyola returned to campus after the first two rounds of the tournament to a rally with 500 students and fans welcoming them home. Players marveled at the turnout compared with some of the tiny audiences they played in front of at Gentile Arena. Students held signs and chanted "L-U-C." "I'm glad they have something to cheer about," Marques Townes said. From the Rogers Park campus throughout the city of Chicago, Loyola inspired an impressive show of support from fans.

7. Final Four Bound

The lasting image from the Elite Eight in Atlanta when Loyola clinched a trip to the Final Four was coach Porter Moser hopping over a press-row table to kiss his wife and hug his four children who had watched from the front row. "Look at this. Are you kidding me?" Moser shouted to the crowd before a net-cutting ceremony. "This is the way it's supposed to be."

John J. Kim/Chicago Tribune

AP Photo/David J. Phillip

8. Selection Sunday

Loyola knew it was in the tournament. It was assured of that after winning the Missouri Valley Conference tournament. But they celebrated like it was breaking news during a watch party with fans at Gentile Arena when the TBS telecast announced "Loyola-Chicago" was set to play Miami in the first round of the tournament in Dallas. Forward Aundre Jackson, a Texas native, called his mom from the stage he sat on with teammates to share the joy.

9. 1963 Support

One row behind Loyola's team bench in the Elite Eight were members of the Ramblers' 1963 national championship team. The only college basketball team from the state of Illinois to ever win a title, the '63 team was forever made iconic by playing in the "Game of Change," which symbolically represented strides to integrate basketball. After the Ramblers beat Kansas State, they officially joined the 1963 team as the only Loyola squads to advance this far in the tournament. Former team captain Jerry Harkness predicted the Ramblers would win it all.

10. Best Buds

After falling 69-57 to No. 3 seed Michigan in the Final Four, Ben Richardson buried his face under his jersey and cried, his arm slung around his best friend and teammate since third grade, Clayton Custer. The two walked down a hallwa at the Missouri Valley Conference tournament in the same manner, only happily recalling how they had won so many games together. This was likely the last time they would play on the same team together. "I'm proud to call him my best friend," Custer said of the senior. ■

John J. Kim/Chicago Tribune

LOOKING BACK

Loyola coach George Ireland, left, poses with players John Egan, Chuck Wood, Ron Miller, Vic Rouse and Leslie Hunter in 1963. (Ed Wagner Jr. / Chicago's American)

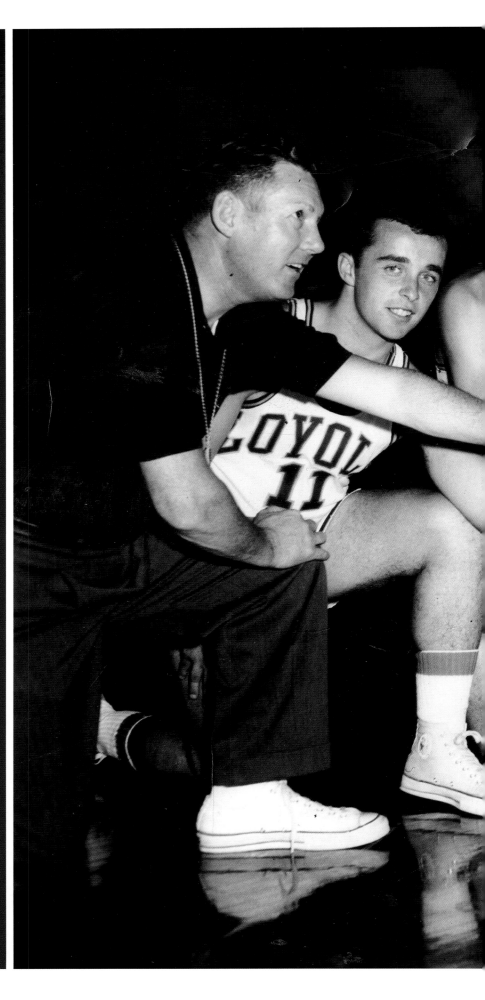

MORE THAN JUST A GAME

1963 Team Known for Winning and Breaking Down Barriers

By Shannon Ryan

L oyola forward Jerry Harkness didn't fully grasp the significance of the game about to be played on March 15, 1963, when he stepped to center court and shook hands with his white opponent.

"I get there and you see these flashbulbs – pop, pop, pop – and I thought, 'Hmm, this is more than a game,' " said Harkness, who is black. "It just felt more like this is history."

The landmark contest later was named the "Game of Change" because it featured an all-white Mississippi State team that defied its state governor's orders banning it from crossing state lines to compete against the integrated Ramblers.

Memories of Loyola's historic role are being recalled as the current Ramblers embark on their first NCAA tournament in 33 years. The squad from 55 years ago won the NCAA tournament championship, the only team from Illinois with that distinction.

Harkness was at center court again celebrating with the 2018 Ramblers in St. Louis as they earned an automatic tournament bid with their Missouri Valley Conference championship. He beamed holding the gold trophy and shaking hands with each player.

Fans give a rousing welcome to the Loyola basketball team as they arrive at O'Hare International Airport in March of 1963. (Chicago Tribune)

"That is the ultimate change, when you talk about integration," Loyola coach Porter Moser said. "As I hugged Jerry Harkness, I told all those guys how much the past is part of our future. The '63 team, that goes way beyond basketball."

Loyola's victory over Mississippi State was symbolic for a country struggling with racial divides and social shifts.

It was a rare team that ignored the unwritten agreement among schools that no more than two black players per team should play at the same time, maybe three if a team trailed significantly. The Ramblers started four black players and sometimes played five.

Coach George Ireland wasn't moved so much by progressive values as winning, players said.

"The idea of starting four was a new experience," said Rich Rochelle, a reserve center. "Five black players at one time, that was unheard of."

Loyola's integrated team – an emblem of equality – inspired abuse from opposing fans and intimidating letters from the Ku Klux Klan.

"It was addressed to my dorm on Sheridan Road," recalled Harkness, a senior captain. "I started thinking, 'These guys are talking like this and they know where we live. What else do they know? They could wait out there and ambush me.' I was afraid."

Team members focused on basketball and academics, but the swirling unrest was hard to ignore in 1963 – the bloodiest year of the Civil Rights Movement.

Four black girls were killed in a Birmingham church bombing. Martin Luther King led the March on Washington and wrote "Letter from a Birmingham Jail." Civil rights activist Medgar Evers was assassinated.

A massive Chicago Public Schools boycott for overcrowding at predominantly African-American schools and a refusal to integrate with white schools made local headlines.

It was the year Alabama Gov. George Wallace exclaimed during his inaugural address, "segregation now, segregation tomorrow, segregation forever."

And here was Loyola – starting four black players and competing against a white team from the South.

"We were in the middle of all of that," Harkness said.

They were about to make another dent in a changing nation.

"That's when it began to turn," center Les Hunter said. "Nobody had ever heard of us and we're showing up with black players and winning like that? It taught people that if you're going to compete, you're going to have to learn acceptance of black athletes."

* * * *

Loyola players were mostly unaware of the game's historic weight.

As the No. 3 team, its most pressing concern was whether its opponent would show for the NCAA tournament regional semifinal game in East Lansing, Mich.

Mississippi Gov. Ross Barnett was a vocal segregationist who forbade the Bulldogs from competing against black players.

But Mississippi State fans had grown tired of staying home while teams like Kentucky competed for trophies. University President Dean Colvard decided to allow the team to play in the tournament anyway – even after Barnett ordered an injunction that barred it from leaving the state.

Colvard devised a plan sending coach Joe "Babe" McCarthy to Memphis as he went to Alabama for a speaking engagement to avoid being served the injunction. An assistant coach sneaked players onto a private plane to Nashville, where they reunited and flew to Michigan where Loyola awaited.

"They were under pressure too," Harkness said.

Before tipoff, Harkness shook hands with forward

Loyola's Billy Smith (24) and Joe Weiss (31) of Santa Clara battle for the rebound during a doubleheader in the 1963 season. (Ed Wagner Jr./Chicago's American)

Joe Dan Gold – and an iconic photo was snapped.

Loyola won 61-51. The contest was without racial incidents. Mississippi State's team returned to a surprisingly welcoming campus. Nobody was fired.

In 2013, Loyola was the first team inducted into the National Collegiate Basketball Hall of Fame and had a White House meeting with President Barack Obama.

"I knew it was important to win, to show superiority on the court and to make a statement that we can play with anybody," Hunter said. "I kind of felt when we ran up the scores on teams that were all white that it was a statement. I was conscious of it."

The "Game of Change" is overshadowed by the 1966 NCAA tournament championship between Texas Western's (now University of Texas at El Paso) five black starters versus an all-white Kentucky team – told in the movie "Glory Road." Even in Chicago, Loyola's season is remembered in black-and-white photographs – a footnote in sports history.

But players' experiences during that season offer a window into the Civil Rights Movement – and reveals their bravery.

* * * *

Houston was particularly hostile. Fans hung over arena railings, screaming racial slurs and launching ice and water as black players entered and exited the court.

In New Orleans, white and black players took separate transportation to games. Rochelle said fans hurled coins at them.

In St. Louis, they were turned away at restaurants.

"One place we went into, sat down and waited and nobody came to us," Rochelle said. "Someone walked in off the street and said, 'We (won't) eat here. They serve (n-----s).' It was not unusual to be treated as second-class citizens. We didn't accept it. But we knew it was there."

Letters from the Klan arrived as word spread about the team with four black starters.

"I can still see Ireland running over to the dorms," Harkness said. "One (letter) said, ' '(Slur) you don't have any right to be playing against white ball players.' It was probably worded tougher than that. Ireland took all the letters and we didn't see them again."

John Egan, the team's white starter, grew up in Marquette Park, a predominantly white South Side neighborhood where in 1966 – three years after Loyola's title – Martin Luther King Jr. marched for equal housing and was struck by rocks as a riot ensued and 30 people were injured.

"When I would come back (to the neighborhood) while I was still in school, they were curious," Egan said. " 'What are you doing on that team?' Then some guys would try to come to my defense, (and say), 'Well, he's the one running the show.' Then I would correct them and say I'm not running the show. The guy playing center (Hunter), the biggest blackest guy on the team, is running the show.' "

Egan said he never had had a black friend, let alone a teammate, before Loyola. The seven surviving teammates remain in touch.

"I didn't know what it would be like to develop a friendship," Egan said. "I think we had a mutual respect."

* * * *

Loyola's championship game against Cincinnati was nearly as momentous as the "Game of Change." With Cincinnati's three black starters, and Harkness, Hunter, Vic Rouse and Ron Miller starting for Loyola, it was the first time the championship featured a majority of black starters.

The defensive-minded Bearcats had won the two previous championships. No. 3-ranked Loyola, which finished 29-2, was a high-scoring squad that

From left to right: Coach George Ireland poses with his championship squad members Vic Rouse, Leslie Hunter, John Egan and Ron Miller. (Phil Mascione/Chicago Tribune)

set a still-standing NCAA record for margin of victory with a 111-42 first-round defeat of Tennessee Tech. In the final at Freedom Hall in Louisville, Loyola rallied from a 15-point deficit for a 60-58 victory in overtime decided on Rouse's last-second put-back of a Hunter miss.

"We could score a whole bunch of points in a short amount of time. I was waiting on that," Hunter said. "I felt it was going to happen. I was always positive about that."

A throng of fans greeted them home at Midway Airport. The team bus arrived on campus as students and Rogers Park neighbors celebrated nearby on Sheridan Road.

"It was the most cheered thing in my life," Harkness said. "It wasn't probably like it is today, but for its time, it was pretty good."

Harkness, who is writing a memoir called "Connections," was inspired to take up basketball as a high school senior thanks to a chance meeting with Jackie Robinson, who complimented him at the Harlem YMCA. Later, Harkness met King and became a civil rights activist.

A consensus first-team All-American as a senior, he also played briefly for the Knicks in the NBA for one season after college and three years later played two seasons with the ABA's Pacers.

Harkness appreciates modern athletes' outspokenness on social issues, seeing a tie to Loyola's 1963 team.

"A person has to look at their strengths and ask, Where can they make a change?" Harkness said. "If we can't voice that things are not right for the average African-American, who will? You do it where it can make a difference. If you're on the stand and you can raise your fist and let people know blacks are not treated right, that makes a difference. And we have that right to do that."

The current political climate hearkens back to the 1960s. Harkness calls events like the white supremacist march in Charlottesville, Va., "painful."

"We've allowed politicians to grab a spotlight that stokes the fires of racism again," Hunter said. "I hate to see some of these things starting up. I don't think America is going to continue to let that stuff happen. It takes awhile for our country to move but it will move in the direction of good."

The '63 team sees its legacy in sports – from college to professional – where players of various races competing together and against each other is the norm.

The players are eager to see how far the current Loyola team can go. The Ramblers (28-5) find out where and against whom they will play when the NCAA tournament brackets are revealed on Selection Sunday.

"I'm absolutely loving it," Rochelle said. "This group of guys is just fantastic. The idea that we were a national championship team from this little commuter school on the North Side of Chicago, it was hard to believe. I hope the same thing happens for this team."

As Loyola reaches the March Madness spotlight, the 1963 team will be remembered as more than former champions.

"You don't realize at the time what you have done – even a little bit – for black-white relations," Harkness said. "That comes later on." ■

Mayor Richard Daley congratulates Coach George Ireland after his Loyola team returns to Chicago with the NCAA championship hardware. (Chicago's American)

1963 NCAA tournament champions Jerry Harkness, from left, Leslie Hunter and John Egan attend the 2018 Sweet 16 game between Loyola and Nevada. (John J. Kim/Chicago Tribune)

THE MARCH TO MADNESS

Cameron Krutwig (25) looks for a pass during Loyola's 65-59 regular season upset over Florida. The Ramblers would triumph in even more memorable victories as the season progressed. (AP Images)

TRIPPIN' OUT

On the Road with the Ramblers

BY TEDDY GREENSTEIN

Carbondale is small-town enough to have Saluki paws painted on its main drag. So a trip to Carbondale's sticks – at night, down a twisty, narrowing road – has Loyola's basketball players hearing the banjo twangs from "Deliverance."

From his front-row seat in the team bus, coach Porter Moser jokes about laying down some marshmallows so the Ramblers can find their way back. Forget Missouri – we're 40 miles from the Kentucky border.

The journey to a dinner spot called "Giant City Lodge" ("Southern Illinois Hospitality at Its Best") is no more unusual, though, than the one the Ramblers have taken this season.

A team that hasn't had a winning conference record since 2007 has ruled the Missouri Valley, claiming the school's first regular-season title in three decades. A brainy school less known than Loyola Academy in some parts of Chicago sold out its arena for a game against Illinois State.

The nav says to take a right at Giant City Lodge Road, but Moser insists it's a left. And he's correct. His sharpshooting players, who entered the weekend ranked No. 1 in the nation at 51.8 percent from the field, have the right guide.

Loyola players added to their cohesiveness and camaraderie during road trips, including this bus ride to Midway Airport for a flight to Marion, Ill., for a game against Southern Illinois. (John J. Kim/Chicago Tribune)

We arrive to be greeted by manager Mikey Kelley, who mentions some canisters of maple syrup contain bourbon.

"Don't you be spiking us!" Moser jokes. "I know you Saluki fans."

The food is prepared upon arrival to maximize efficiency, and it is a feast: perfectly crisp fried chicken, waffles, dumplings, potatoes and gravy, corn and cole slaw. Water is the beverage of choice for Moser, who says he never would drink alcohol in front of a player.

Beneath a mounted elk head, the table talk centers around current college coaches who played in the NBA, starting with Georgetown's Patrick Ewing and Chris Mullin of St. John's. (We did not forget about Bryce Drew and Kevin Ollie, Bulls fans.)

Before the plates clear, a waiter sidles up to Moser and discreetly tells him dessert is not included in the cost of the meal. Would he like to add an offering of cheesecake for his 29-man party? Maybe cobbler? Moser says yes to the cobbler.

The waiter returns: Would he approve a scoop of ice cream for the cobbler?

The table goes quiet. It's a bit awkward, like rummaging through a stranger's wallet to find his ID.

Moser says yes and then cracks: "When we were winning 15 games, no a la mode."

Times are good for the school sandwiched between Lake Michigan and the Red Line. The Ramblers have a coach whom the athletic director describes as "perfect," a man who knows there's more to the job than switching from man to zone defense.

Among his decisions: take a bus or spring for a charter flight? Spend leftover funds on travel or recruiting?

Moser has twice raised $150,000 to take his team on overseas trips and has had six assistant coaches poached by Power Five programs.

This isn't the life of every mid-major coach. But it is the way for Moser, who manages the bottom line while his team hunts for an NCAA tournament bid and his players maintain a collective 3.1 GPA.

Tuesday 1:30 p.m. | 'People care'

The plan had been to practice from 3 to 5 p.m. before busing to Midway for a charter flight to Carbondale. But a flight crew got sick, necessitating that everything be moved up 3 1/2 hours.

"Just another something to roll with," Moser says.

Loyola would improve to 24-5 on its trip to Southern Illinois, during which Moser gave the Tribune access to the team charter, bus rides, meals, a video session, the shootaround, walk-through and postgame locker room.

It was there, after his team trounced the Salukis, that Moser had his players howling while he unbuttoned his dress shirt to reveal a T-shirt heralding the Ramblers as conference champions.

"People care about Loyola basketball again," athletic director Steve Watson says, "and that has been a lot of fun."

Less fun will come when the final horn sounds on Loyola's season. A year ago, everyone asked Northwestern athletic director Jim Phillips: How will you keep Chris Collins? Watson is getting the same questions.

"What's nice is he loves it here, his family loves it here and we love having him here," Watson says. "He has the perfect background – grew up in Chicago, Catholic high school (Benet), played in the Valley (Creighton), Jesuit school. What makes him even more special is his enthusiasm – nobody has to tell him, 'Hey, go thank the band; thank the cheerleaders.' He does that, and it's 100 percent sincere.

"We'll do everything we can to figure out a way to make sure he is here for a long time. We joke about it a little bit."

Watson recalls the time Moser spoke to a fan/

Loyola center Carson Shanks (left) and Aundre Jackson depart the Giant City Lodge restaurant in Makanda, Ill., during the Southern Illinois road trip. (John J. Kim/Chicago Tribune)

alumni group. The coach gushed about his athletic director. Watson took the floor and said, "Yeah, Porter is always negotiating for his next contract."

Watson felt awful, texting Moser to say the comment should have remained a joke between the two. Moser was OK with it and says the two have a very good relationship.

Moser, 49, is believed to make $420,000, which ranks in the top half among Missouri Valley coaches. Ben Jacobson is an outlier, having turned down numerous lucrative jobs to stay at Northern Iowa, which pays him $900,000.

Middle class in the Big Ten is north of $2 million per year. Northwestern lavished Collins with a $3 million-a-year deal.

Moser lives in Wilmette and has four kids at Catholic schools, two at Loyola Academy.

"I'm not even thinking about the next step," he says. "Honest to God, I have put my whole life, sweat and tears into this (job), and it has not been easy. It's fun to see from where we came to where we are. I'm so much in the moment with this group, I don't even want to think about other things."

4 p.m. | 'This is dope!'

The team bus is averaging about 1 mph on Lake Shore Drive as rain pours down. The smiling Waze logo is probably laughing.

Several players, glued to their phones or tablets, are hollering. House of Highlights on Instagram?

Nah, they're watching Chelsea and Barcelona play to a 1-1 draw.

Loyola's top two scorers are in the back, and both have interesting back stories.

Marques Townes' favorite word is "Jersey" – the state, not the uniform. He's from New Jersey, played high school ball in Jersey with Karl-Anthony Towns (Timberwolves) and Wade Baldwin (Trail Blazers)

and went to a Jersey college, Fairleigh Dickinson. He started as a sophomore for a team that reached the NCAA tournament, scoring 13 points in a blowout loss to Florida Gulf Coast.

And then the Jersey kid did the unthinkable: He transferred to a place he barely knew.

"I'd never heard of Loyola, to be honest," Townes says. "I knew Loyola Marymount but didn't know there was one in Chicago. I started looking into it, saw the campus was on the lake and thought: Oh, this is dope! This is nice. They were heavy on me right away. They did a tremendous job recruiting me."

Moser and his staff homed in on another transfer, Clayton Custer, the moment they heard he was leaving Iowa State and Fred Hoiberg.

Moser flew to Ames to eat with Custer at Hickory Park barbecue – and then drove nearly four hours to Overland Park, Kan., to chat up Custer's parents.

The time investment was well worth it: The 6-foot-1 Custer is averaging 14.7 points and is in the Missouri Valley's top five in field-goal percentage (56.4), 3-point percentage (49), free-throw percentage (80.6), assists (4.1) and steals (1.7).

He and Hoiberg, whom Custer calls a "brilliant offensive mind," left for Chicago at about the same time.

Asked if he presses his former coach for Bulls tickets, Custer smiles and says the NCAA doesn't allow it.

"If it were not (illegal)," he says, "I'd be hitting him up all the time."

4:25 p.m. | 'No. 1 for takeoff'

As the bus rolls into an area of Midway used for private aviation, the players debate which plane will transport them.

"We've got to be rockin' the Air Canada," one says.

No, this will be a more modest one, as on most trips. It has 30 seats and a 1-2 seating layout with standard leg room.

Porter Moser paces alongside Loyola players during practice for their game against Southern Illinois in Carbondale. (John J. Kim/Chicago Tribune)

"I'll sit on Ben's lap," Custer jokes of his teammate and friend since childhood, Ben Richardson.

A flight attendant named Robin announces: "We're going to Marion (Ill.) to beat SIU."

Says the captain: "We're grads of Purdue but wish you the best. No. 1 for takeoff."

The flight lasts 55 minutes. The drive from Loyola to Midway took twice that long.

6:30 p.m. | 'Big Time Where You Are'

After a brief stop at what Moser calls "the nicest hotel in Carbondale" – the Holiday Inn – the team rides the bus for 15 minutes to SIU Arena, the generically named home of the Salukis.

"I hit a bomb here," Moser says, recalling a moment from the 1988-89 season when he stroked a 26-footer (the shot gets a foot longer with each retelling) to put his Creighton team up by four.

Not every road team visits the arena the night before a game, but Moser says his players "love to shoot." That can be an issue at Loyola, which has only one gym, Gentile Arena, for the games and practices of four teams: men's and women's hoops, men's and women's volleyball.

"That has been one of the biggest challenges in turning this around," Moser says. "These guys want to shoot all the time, and there's always a team practicing there."

Good news: The school announced Feb. 5 that the Alfie Norville Practice Facility will be constructed on campus and will open in the summer of 2019. Moser appreciates Loyola's improved commitment, recalling a 2001 book he read by a football coach named Frosty Westering titled, "Make the Big Time Where You Are."

"That's our mentality," Moser says. "I don't spend my energy bitching. I spend my energy trying to make it big-time for these guys."

Last season highlighted the perils of operating under a modest travel budget. Rather than pay about $35,000 for a round-trip charter, the Ramblers bused six hours to Carbondale, losing to SIU by two points. Then they bused back. Days later they bused to St. Louis for the MVC tournament, losing again to the Salukis by five.

"Chartering is a big deal," Moser says.

The Ramblers take full advantage, hoisting shots for 45 minutes. Then it's on to the team dinner at Giant City Lodge, a meal that also would not have been possible if a bus had delivered them to Carbondale at, say, 9 p.m.

"Watch Custer's stroke," Moser says, turning the conversation back to basketball. "It comes out so easy."

And of 6-9 freshman center Cameron Krutwig: "He is like a 5-8 walk-on. He loves to play. You don't see too many centers who are gym rats."

9:40 p.m. Tuesday | 'Body blows'

The Holiday Inn's ballrooms are under construction, so the players, coaches and staff stuff into a fourth-floor room to watch film.

"All right, men, it's obviously a little hot in here," Moser says, "but you have to bear with it."

On the walls are a dozen hand-diagrammed SIU plays with A/B/C sequences. Moser uses a laser pointer as assistant coach Matt "Flash" Gordon selects plays from an Apple laptop for the projector screen.

"He's 25 percent from 3," Gordon says of one Saluki. "We want him taking contested 3s."

Says Moser: "There has been a point in the second half (of games) where we get teams to break. It has been the body blows."

Wednesday 10 a.m. | 'Can't throw those away'

As players visit the buffet in the hotel restaurant for the standard fare of French toast, cereal, eggs and bacon, the coaches huddle in a booth with their

The Loyola Ramblers line up for the national anthem at SIU Arena. (John J. Kim/Chicago Tribune)

laptops open. The game-planning never ends.

"You know how in some years you win all the close games?" Moser says of SIU, which has won two straight in overtime. "It's uncanny."

Townes is wearing shorts as he arrives on the team bus at 10:45. It's 35 degrees and raining – a 35-degree drop since Tuesday night.

"This weather is acting totally different," he says.

Assistant coach Bryan Mullins used to wear Salukis maroon before shifting to the maroon favored by the Ramblers.

"I have a few NCAA (tournament) T-shirts," he says on the ride to the arena. "Can't throw those away."

Mullins, in his fifth year working for Moser, chose SIU after a Hall of Fame career at Downers Grove South High School because of, he says, "the tradition and the winning – and I knew they needed a point guard."

He has fondness for his alma mater, of course, but says "it would be awesome to celebrate a (Missouri Valley) championship here."

11:55 a.m. | 'Squeeze it'

Moser concludes his detailed walk-through by having his 10 rotation players sit in folding chairs under a basket. He adopted this from mentor Rick Majerus.

Moser is animated as he gets low into a defensive stance, shuffling his feet with his arms extended. He looks like the last guy in the world one would want to guard in a rec-league game, but he rarely plays pickup after having blown out his Achilles tendon.

"Now it's time to get locked in on all the little things," Moser says. "Our best offense is what?"

"Our defense!" the players respond.

Moser: "You have to go after every rebound with two hands because they're coming."

SIU leads the conference in steals – and Moser is determined not to allow a Saluki to poke the ball free after

Clockwise from bottom left: Loyola Ramblers players Donte Ingram, Adarius Avery, Carson Shanks and Marques Townes eat a breakfast of champions prior to the Southern Illinois game. (John J. Kim/Chicago Tribune)

a Loyola rebound.

"Squeeze it after a free throw," he says as his players huddle up. Hands in. "One, two, three ... Team together!"

12:40 p.m. | 'Still haven't found ...'

Like many in his all-consuming profession, Moser does not sleep well. Coaches have a wealth of digital clips, and they're accessible on a tablet they can take to bed.

"It's so easy to flip around," he says.

Moser stayed up late watching SIU force 20 Loyola turnovers during the teams' first meeting, a 14-point Ramblers victory. Then he watched how Valparaiso guarded SIU's plays. Then he analyzed the final five minutes of the Salukis' overtime victories.

He slept about five hours, in chunks.

Even on bus trips or flights, he rarely vegges out to music. His favorite band is U2, his favorite song "I Still Haven't Found What I'm Looking For."

That's my wedding song, I tell him.

5:12 p.m. | 'Night and day'

This bus ride to the arena is totally unlike the previous ones.

"Night and day," says Bill Behrns, Loyola's athletic communications chief.

Not a word is spoken.

7:21 p.m. | 'You can't let up'

Moser wasn't lying: His guys love to shoot. And they miss less often than any team in the country.

After seven minutes at SIU Arena, the score is Ramblers 21, Salukis 8. Loyola is 8 of 10 from the field and has hit 5 of 6 from 3-point range.

But Moser is wary.

"They almost got Donte (Ingram) on the poke down there," he says of a near turnover under Loyola's basket.

With SIU creeping back, Moser says to his players on the bench: "Hey, we need stops! Talk to them, fellas."

Townes fires a pass into the seats and taps himself, acknowledging the error.

"See," Moser says, "you can't let up."

Later in the first half, the refs whistle Aundre Jackson for a foul on an SIU drive.

"That's terrible!" Moser says of the call. "Great verticality, Aundre!"

Custer turns it over with a forced pass into the paint at the end of the half but knocks down a 3 to open the second.

The Ramblers pull away, with Moser calling for a "long possession" time and again down the stretch.

The final score is Loyola 75, SIU 56. The Ramblers have just run the Valley's No. 2 team out of its own gym to clinch the conference's solo crown.

8:53 p.m. | 'I'll never forget it'

"Heavenly father," Moser says during the postgame prayer in the locker room. "We thank you for the incredible group we have here. We thank you for the gifts you've given us. We know that by your grace and glory we've come together. We've persevered, we've worked hard, we give all the glory to you. We give thanks and praise. In your name we pray."

Then Moser stands in front of his players and says: "I'm really, really proud of you."

And then he plucks a story from his playing days at Creighton. The year was 1989.

"We went on the road to Drake and we had to win (to) get the outright (title)," Moser tells them. "(Coach) Tony Barone sat in front of us, I'll never forget it. And the (expletive) wore a championship shirt ..."

Moser can't get out another word. His players mob him.

Yes, this has been a lot of fun. ∎

Head coach Porter Moser addresses Loyola players at practice before the Southern Illinois contest. The Ramblers would go on to beat the Salukis 75-56. (John J. Kim/Chicago Tribune)

REGULAR SEASON
FEBRUARY 3, 2018 · CHICAGO, ILLINOIS
LOYOLA 97, MISSOURI STATE 75

MAKING SOME NOISE

Buzzworthy Ramblers look like contender for NCAA tournament bid

By Teddy Greenstein

Loyola coach Porter Moser did two things upon entering the interview room after his team's rousing home victory over Missouri State.

One, he switched chairs, dispatching the sweat-infused one that guard Clayton Custer used.

Two, he thanked the 3,592 souls who gave Gentile Arena a terrific vibe.

"We've been starving," Moser said, "for atmospheres like that."

It was raucous. Students formed a mini whiteout by wearing white Ts, and they hollered "L-U-C!" throughout and "You let the whole team down!" after Missouri State missed free throws.

But Moser wants more. And this Loyola team deserves more.

On a day with no football to watch, with Illinois, Northwestern and UIC idle, there were still nearly 1,000 empty seats in this modern, intimate arena to witness a Ramblers team improve to 19-5 against the preseason favorites of the Missouri Valley.

"The goal is to fill that thing up, to have a major ticket problem," Moser said. "This shows you how loud it can get. Can you imagine it with another thousand?"

Three conference home games remain for a program that has by far the best chance of any team in the state to make the NCAA tournament. (Projected as a No. 12 seed in Joe Lunardi's latest ESPN bracket, Loyola probably needs to win the Valley tournament to get there. At 9-3 in the Valley with six games left, the Ramblers are in prime position for its No. 1 seed.)

If you dig teams with unselfish players and a free-flowing offense, carve out some time for the Ramblers.

Loyola entered the game second in the nation in home field-goal percentage. But that 54.4 percent mark wasn't satisfactory for these Ramblers, so they hit 15 of their first 20 attempts. They ended up shooting 60.9 percent with 24 assists to nine turnovers in their 97-75 victory. Their home field-goal percentage rose to 55.1 percent, best in the nation over Michigan State (54.7 percent).

"It shows how we have bought into coach's system," guard Marques Townes said. "Being connected and being together with a big emphasis on sharing the ball."

Lead guard Clayton Custer scored a game-high 23 points on 9-for-11 shooting and added six assists. But with Loyola, it's never about one guy. Six scored in double figures.

"We want pace and space and not letting the ball stick," Moser said.

The crowd included Bulls executive vice president John Paxson and 12 other NBA scouts, all of whom came to see Alize Johnson, the 6-foot-9 senior who entered averaging 15.3 points and 11.5 boards for Missouri State.

He had a decent showing with 14 and 9, threading a perfect pass for a transition layup and one of his five assists.

The Ramblers provided the real show, though, hitting the 50-point mark with 4:21 left in the first half.

"Amazing," Custer said of the atmosphere. "We want more and more people to come out."

Townes then leaned into the mic: "Tell the people in Chicago to come to Loyola basketball." ∎

Loyola senior Donte Ingram grabs one of his six rebounds in the victory against Missouri State. (John J. Kim/Chicago Tribune)

REGULAR SEASON
FEBRUARY 21, 2018 · CARBONDALE, ILLINOIS
LOYOLA 75, SOUTHERN ILLINOIS 56

CLAIMING CONFERENCE CROWN

Win Over Salukis Nails Down 1st Outright Title Since 1987

BY TEDDY GREENSTEIN

Loyola coach Porter Moser took the floor wearing the gray patterned blazer that brought good luck during the team's stunning early-season victory at Florida.

And his Ramblers took the court at Southern Illinois hoping to turn a "co-" into a "solo."

After clinching a share of the Missouri Valley regular-season title at Evansville, this game against the league's No. 2 team represented the Ramblers' chance to win it outright.

And that they did, blitzing the Salukis with great shooting (57.4 percent) and ballhandling (18 assists). The 75-56 win gives Loyola (24-5, 14-3) its first regular-season solo conference title since it won the Midwestern Collegiate Conference (now Horizon League) in 1987.

"Our guys talked about getting (rid) of the 'co-,'" Moser said. "I really sensed it at Evansville. It wasn't fake. The guys said let's hold off on celebrating."

The Ramblers will return home to their first full house since 2003, as the school announced that Saturday's game against Illinois State is a sellout. The Ramblers are averaging just 2,222 fans at the 4,963-seat Gentile Arena.

Moser anticipated a raucous crowd Wednesday at SIU Arena, so he had crowd noise piped into practice Tuesday so the Ramblers could practice non-verbal communication.

Turns out that hand signals were not needed. Loyola raced out to a 21-8 lead, hitting 8 of 10 from the field, including 5 of 6 on 3-pointers.

Clayton Custer led the way with 16 points, and Ben Richardson had eight assists without a turnover. Kavion Pippen, the 6-foot-10 nephew of Scottie Pippen, scored 16 points to lead SIU. ∎

Loyola junior Clayton Custer, who scored a team-high 16 points against Southern Illinois, attempts a shot against Salukis guard Armon Fletcher. (John J. Kim/Chicago Tribune)

REGULAR SEASON

FEBRUARY 24, 2018 · CHICAGO, ILLINOIS

LOYOLA 68, ILLINOIS STATE 61

A PROMISE OF MORE IN STORE

Ramblers Reward Sellout Home Crowd with 25th Victory

By Teddy Greenstein

There was plenty of nervous energy in the gym during Loyola's final home game.

Loyola had finally arrived at the big time – a conference crown, ESPN2 broadcasting from a sold-out Gentile Arena – and the Ramblers looked jittery.

They air-balled 3s and fumbled routine passes. Favored by a dozen points over Illinois State, they led by just one with two minutes to play.

Then Ben Richardson made a 3. And his best friend since the third grade, fellow Loyola guard Clayton Custer, ended his 0-for-9 dry spell with a bomb.

"That's why I love this team," Custer said. "We always have each other's backs."

Loyola dominated the final stretch and walked off with a 68-61 victory, prompting an on-court celebration that included the cutting of the nets before a crowd of 4,963.

"A sold-out crowd on my last day here is so special," Richardson, a senior, hollered into the mic. "And we have a lot more in store for you guys!"

Up next is Arch Madness and, Loyola hopes, March Madness.

Despite a 25-5 record (15-3 in the Missouri Valley) and top-35 RPI, the Ramblers will go on the assumption they must win the league tournament in St. Louis to make the NCAAs. That's what the bracketologists believe, citing Loyola's nonconference schedule rank of 271.

"This is definitely not the finish line," Loyola coach Porter Moser said after the win over ISU. "I want them to enjoy it, but we know there's another level we need to get to, and it will take a harder effort." ∎

Throughout the regular season and postseason, Loyola and its scarf-wearing band members captured the hearts of those around Chicago and the country. (John J. Kim/Chicago Tribune)

HEAD COACH

PORTER MOSER

No Sleep Till May

By Teddy Greenstein

You don't need GPS to find Porter Moser's home in Wilmette. Just follow the red-brick road until you come upon the toilet paper.

Friends and neighbors, drunk on Loyola's unbelievable Final Four run, turned the Mosers' front yard into something you'd see if a tornado tore through a Charmin factory.

Not that the family minds. Porter, wife Megan, daughter Jordan, 16, and sons Jake, 15, Ben, 13, and Max, 11, are loving the attention as much as the Ramblers love sharing the basketball.

The other day Jordan was pumping gas when she noticed Loyola highlights on the little TV screen and nearly fainted: "Mom!" she shouted. "Look!"

There's no too-cool-for-school vibe in this cheery house, where Moser's Missouri Valley Conference coach of the year trophy rests, for now, on the dining room table.

Just six weeks earlier, the Ramblers played before a home crowd generously listed at 2,091.

Now?

"How cool is this?" Moser said, pointing at a NIT game on the living room TV. "Nonstop Loyola stuff is coming up (on the crawl)."

Moser shared a picture of his parents' grave site in Naperville. Near some flowers, a fan posted laminated images of Loyola's wolf mascot and the NCAA 2018 Final Four insignia.

Moser also marveled at how "GO LOYOLA" was spelled out in lights across the top of the Blue Cross-Blue Shield Tower on Lake Shore Drive.

"I remember seeing 'GO CUBS,'" he said of his favorite professional team.

The Ramblers are so old-school, Moser said they have no dunks through four tournament games. They're so team-oriented, they most likely have no future NBA players.

As shocking as their run through four higher-seeded teams has been, Moser's lifelong friends and longtime admirers are not surprised with his success.

Blackhawks executive vice president Jay Blunk recalled how his fellow Wilmette resident would tell him: "'We're building something. We have this great little arena and we will great this place rockin'. I want

Coach Porter Moser encourages his team during practice prior to Loyola's first-round upset of Miami. (John J. Kim/Chicago Tribune)

to show it to you.' ... Porter is different. He's sincere and has a genuine interest in you. He draws you in, and you're hooked."

Said Bulls general manager Gar Forman, who coached at Iowa State when Moser was at Texas A&M in the late 1990s. "He just gets it. His drive to succeed, his work ethic, his intensity. You can spot which guys will make it and which ones will fall to the side."

Todd Eisner, a college coach who played with Moser at Creighton in the late '80s, told his friend recently: "I know you're getting only 2-3 hours of sleep a night. When this is over, you're gonna need to hibernate."

Moser replied: "No, I need to be on the road recruiting."

Told that story, Moser noted the arduous April recruiting calendar and said: "I'll sleep in May."

* * * *

Don't get the wrong idea about Moser, who turns 50 in August. Only part of him admires Nick Saban, the Alabama football coach who called recruits within hours of winning the 2016 national title.

"Now that is obsessive," Moser said, "and I'm 100 percent not that guy."

The well-rounded Moser is either an incredible husband and father, or Megan and their kids can teach Meryl Streep a thing or two about acting.

All four were wearing Loyola gear Tuesday night, and Moser had to laugh when Max described his tightly wound dad as "cool" and "chill."

They all play travel basketball, and Jordan said she actually enjoys the rides home from games: "I'll say, 'How do you think I did?' He says: 'I thought you rebounded really well, but on defense make sure you use your legs to get in a slide.' It's always a bunch of positives, the coolest balance. I don't feel a lot of pressure from him. I love getting the inside tips."

Moser is so clean-cut that he half-jokingly declined to confirm that Miller Lite is his favorite beer. And after it was revealed that he and Megan met at a Texas A&M bar where she served drinks, he called the spot "an establishment."

He emerged from the basement with this offering of drinks: "I have Diet 7UP, diet cranberry, water and Gatorade."

He served orange Gatorade on the rocks in a Jake Arrieta souvenir Cubs cup.

Said Megan: "He loves his job. I know there are days that are terrible and days that are great. He comes home from traveling for three days and watching film till 1 in the morning and says: 'OK, let's play some games, go to dinner ... what do you guys want to do?' Basically, he's just so fun."

Friends say Megan is as crucial to Moser's success as the man himself.

"We're partners in everything," Moser said. "People talk about me having high energy. She has a glow that makes you feel good to be around. I don't want to say she's one of the guys ..."

Megan: "That's fine."

Porter: "She can talk sports, drink a beer with the guys, kid with them. I'll go out with the guys and the next think you know, they're mingling with her.

"I've talked to so many coaches who say: 'My wife is killing me about my job; she says I'm gone too much.' We've been married over 20 years and I'm not exaggerating. Not one time has she complained about my job. She is 100 percent all-in, so understanding.

"I'll get back from a three-day trip, and she'll have a meal waiting for me. And when you have a partnership like that, I'll try to take something off her plate – I'll race from Loyola to pick one of them up from AAU practice."

Megan: "You fill in the gaps instead of keeping score."

Porter: "That's a great line."

Wait, is there also a Wall of Culture in the Moser

A Rick Majerus disciple, Porter Moser can get fiery, as he did after a first-half call during the Elite Eight. (John J. Kim/Chicago Tribune)

home? Sort of. There's a family group chat on which Moser posts inspirational quotes or links to inspiring stories.

Jordan can quote her dad's favorite line about the scourge of self-pity: "How you think is how you feel, how you feel is how you act, and how you act is what defines you."

This is a man who, to help his kids wake up in the morning, created a Spotify mix with songs that contain the word "happy" in the title.

This was a boy who provided so much light, his mother, Sandy, would see him and say: "Here comes 'Sunshine.'"

Sandy so often stressed the need for a "positive mental attitude" that "PMA" became a family mantra. It's also how Moser monograms his shirts.

"I have horrible initials," he explained. "My middle name is Andrew."

* * * *

Normally on the Friday preceding the Final Four, Moser and coaching buddies such as Eisner (Division II Winona State in Minnesota) and Phil LaScala (Lake Forest High School) embark on a mission to find the perfect sports bar to watch the Saturday semifinals.

"Never the popular places," Eisner said. "We want to watch the games and hear the TV announcers, not be somewhere crowded and noisy. Unfortunately our minds never turn off. We want to see what the teams are running, so we find a hole-in-the-wall spot with a lot of TVs and cold beer."

Eisner joked that he will feel like "a lost puppy" in San Antonio because Moser "ruined the trip by taking his team to the Final Four."

He added: "I've never been more excited for a game."

Moser, Eisner and Matt Roggenburk formed the Tony Barone's first full recruiting class at Creighton.

Moser arrived as a walk-on but never acted as if he were lacking anything.

"He woke up every day saying: 'I will prove I belong here and earn a scholarship,'" Eisner said. "That fire you see from him now is what we saw when he was 18 years old ... He was an unbelievable shooter. He had a torch, as my players would say. He could really stroke it from deep and he would fight you (on defense). But he was not the most gifted athlete and had a two-dribble limit."

Moser said it was more like a zero-dribble limit. Players would hand off to him in the layup line.

He and LaScala formed a backcourt at Benet Academy that helped maintain the school's 102-game home winning streak from 1975-87.

"He would always have the boombox, playing everything from Michael Jackson to Ozzy Osbourne before and after practices and games," LaScala said. "That thing was huge."

Moser naturally stood out as a rising ninth-grader at Ray Meyer's summer camp. In front of all the campers, Meyer had Moser stand up and announced: "If everyone worked as hard as this kid ... I guarantee he will get a college scholarship."

Added LaScala: "We were like, 'Whoa!'"

LaScala spent the week on a Mexican cruise that docks at Galveston, Texas. Needless to say, he will make it to San Antonio.

So will Eisner, who said he normally has access to tickets that require binoculars to see the floor. Not this time. Not with the best man at his wedding coaching against Michigan in the first game.

"I've been going to the Final Four for 27 years," Moser said. "It's a great time to see friends in the profession in a more social atmosphere. But I can tell you unequivocally that I'm so happy that I'm going to prepare and compete."

He can sleep in May. ∎

Coach Porter Moser arrives on the Loyola campus after defeating Kansas State to reach the Final Four.
(Armando L. Sanchez/Chicago Tribune)

TEAM CHAPLAIN

SISTER JEAN

Loyola's Face to the World

BY SHANNON RYAN

On a sunny day between opening-round games of the NCAA men's basketball tournament in Dallas, Loyola's 98-year-old team chaplain, Sister Jean Dolores Schmidt, planned to go for a simple lunch down the street.

"We couldn't do it – everybody knows her," said Tom Hitcho, the university's longtime senior associate athletic director for operations, who has been pushing Sister Jean's wheelchair during the tournament.

They were stopped so frequently by adoring fans on the sidewalk, it was nearly impossible to make it more than a few steps before another one approached. They opted to return to the hotel for lunch.

Even at the hotel, people in town for a convention – not for basketball – knew Sister Jean. She's in so many selfies, she now prepares to pose.

Ah, the life of a national celebrity.

Actually, let Sister Jean correct that.

"International celebrity," she quipped to a TV news reporter. She mentioned being the subject of news segments in Mexico and Britain.

Darren Rovell, ESPN's sports business reporter, said Sister Jean has been tweeted about more than any other person connected with any team during the NCAA tournament. (Sorry, Donte Ingram and Clayton Custer, the Loyola players who hit game-winning shots in the first and second rounds.)

NBC's "Access" interviewed the California native Monday and called her the "biggest star of the tournament."

In an interview via Skype with the entertainment program, she deflected praise and lauded the team: "I think the stardom rests with the coach and with the team. I'm sort of in the background doing the hard pushing. They're the ones that do the playing and get the credit."

Loyola's popularity during this tournament isn't due only to dramatic shots and impressive upsets. Sister Jean, the team chaplain since 1994, has had a TV camera trained on her during games and has been mic'd up for her pregame prayers.

A former player and coach, she knows her

Fans take photos of Sister Jean Dolores Schmidt, who has become a media sensation during the tournament, after Loyola defeated Kansas State. (Armando L. Sanchez/Chicago Tribune)

basketball and provides comforting words and feedback to players after each game.

She grew up in San Francisco and joined the Sisters of Charity of the Blessed Virgin Mary convent in Iowa after high school. She returned to California, where she taught school and coached basketball for 20 years before taking a teaching job in 1961 at Mundelein College.

Not long after the all-women's school merged with Loyola in 1991, Sister Jean retired from the education department. She was asked to replace the retiring chaplain of the men's basketball team and has held the post for 24 years.

Loyola has been cognizant of Sister Jean's health on the trips.

After missing nine games this season – a rarity during her tenure – because of a broken hip, she returned late in the season to watch home games in the tunnel from her wheelchair.

She insisted on traveling with the team to St. Louis for the Missouri Valley Conference tournament, which the Ramblers won to earn their NCAA tournament berth. A nurse accompanied her to St. Louis, and a wellness center employee traveled with her to Dallas.

She said all the attention is deserved for the team and good for Loyola.

"I think everybody is a celebrity in his and her own way," she told "Access." "No matter what we do, if we're doing what we're supposed to be doing, then each one of us is a celebrity, each one is bright in the eyes of God."

About 500 fans greeted the Ramblers when they returned to campus after their first two NCAA tournament games in Dallas. Sister Jean was cheered as loudly as any player when coming off the bus.

"I think it's wonderful that they were there," she said. "I was hoping some of them would be there to greet the team because the team deserves that. And the students deserve to celebrate.

"And when I saw them there, I just became so emotional. ... That shows the spirit of Loyola, and we want to continue that."

Loyola has received dozens of national media requests for Sister Jean. Local reporters are rushing to catch up with a woman who has been a campus icon for decades.

Sister Jean, who lives in a freshman dormitory, is popular at Loyola but isn't treated like a novelty. She's just beloved.

Cheerleaders wave to her. Students pop in for chats at her office in the student center. Campus administrators recognize her for her years of selfless service to the community. Athletes from multiple sports shower her with hugs.

"You brought that magic," Custer told her on the court at the American Airlines Center after the Ramblers beat Miami.

Sister Jean said she will continue to pray for the well-being of the players and, yes, for more Loyola victories.

And she'll enjoy the Ramblers' ride.

She had the same thought that likely popped into many Loyola fans' minds the morning after Custer's shot with 3.6 seconds left beat Tennessee and sent the Ramblers to the Sweet 16 for the first time since 1985.

"Oh," she said she told herself. "It's not a dream." ■

At 98 years of age, Sister Jean Dolores Schmidt is having the time of her life during Loyola's postseason run. (Armando L. Sanchez/Chicago Tribune)

FOREVER HITCHED TO LOYOLA SPORTS

Whatever the Problem, Longtime Administrator Hitcho Will Handle It

BY DAVID HAUGH

As Loyola coach Porter Moser cut down the nets at Philips Arena in Atlanta after clinching a spot in the Final Four, he remembered one thing before stepping down the ladder.

Everything good at Loyola comes with a "Hitch."

So Moser snipped a piece of the net and presented it to Tom Hitcho, affectionately called "Hitch," the beloved longtime Loyola senior associate athletic director who more than one staffer referred to as "the heart and soul of the athletic department."

"That was very gracious of Porter," said Hitcho, 69.

Even before Sister Jean Dolores Schmidt became Loyola's team chaplain in 1994, Hitcho had established himself as the go-to guy for athletes and administrators, the last man hired by legendary coach and athletic director George Ireland and the first person everyone looks to for answers. At Loyola since 1977, Hitcho represents a historical bridge between the Ireland era and the Moser renaissance, an invaluable resource who does everything for every sport, from taping ankles to planning trips to just plain listening.

"The Swiss army knife of our department," said Bill Behrns, Loyola's assistant athletic director. "We've always said when Hitch leaves, we're in trouble because he's the glue to this place. At some point in his career, he's taken on any and every role."

Hitcho's latest role has cast him as the Morgan Freeman of Loyola sports, pushing Sister Jean in her wheelchair with care the way Freeman chauffeured Jessica Tandy in "Driving Miss Daisy." As Sister Jean's international celebrity grew, Loyola needed somebody the 98-year-old nun trusted to navigate the maze of fans and media at NCAA tournament sites in Dallas and Atlanta.

Enter Hitcho, the gentlemanly dear friend of Sister Jean's who visited her regularly after she broke her hip and even brought dinner some nights to make life easier. Hitcho's presence amid the chaos offers Sister Jean a comfortable voice leading the way alongside three bodyguards and two nurses.

"We have to take care of our guardian angel," Hitcho said. "It's like a snowball effect in a good way. But everyone is so gracious – fans, security guards, opposing teams. She's so intelligent, so smart, and understands people and society. She's such a unique person, a breath of freshness. Everybody loves her."

Funny, Loyola athletes from all sports and eras say the same thing about Hitcho, a member of Loyola's Hall of Fame who had a training room dedicated in his name in 2012. Behrns says the first thing ex-players of all ages ask when they visit the Loyola athletic office is: "Where's Hitch?" At Saturday's victory over Kansas State, Hitcho likened it to a reunion with all the former Ramblers present and posed for pictures with everyone who asked, including two who flew in from China:

More than just the man who pushes Sister Jean's wheelchair, Tom "Hitch" Hitcho is a beloved figure in Loyola athletics. (John J. Kim/Chicago Tribune)

Matt Jung and Donyale Bush.

"The thing about Hitch is he's got a little Sister Jean in him, the male version of her around here," Behrns said. "He is so adored by every student-athlete that comes through and has an unbelievable ability to still relate to college kids incredibly well."

Added Moser: "I love Hitch."

The feeling is mutual, and Hitcho still laughs sharing his favorite example of Moser's exuberance. A couple of years ago during a CBI tournament game, Moser protested an official's call with such vigor that he ran a few rows into the bleachers. The ref called a technical foul.

"Now the NCAA officiating team uses that as a visual of what not to do as a coach," Hitcho said with a chuckle.

Moser is the seventh coach Hitcho has worked with. He came to Loyola from Indiana State, one of the few schools that offered a graduate degree in athletic training. The native of Duquesne, Pa., earned his bachelor's degree at Youngstown State and served four years in the Navy after graduation, courtesy of the draft. Serving his country exposed Hitcho to the world, flying reconnaissance missions over Europe, Cuba, Africa and the Middle East. The guy who gets along with everybody seemingly has been everywhere.

He sought more stability after completing his service and landed at Indiana State, where he taped Larry Bird's ankles before practices his first season as a Sycamore. A year later, Ireland was looking for a good trainer at Loyola, and Dr. Bob Behnke, Hitcho's professor at Indiana State, recommended him and he was off to Chicago.

His first season proved memorable. Loyola beat second-ranked Marquette, Bird's Indiana State team and coach John Thompson's Georgetown Hoyas at Alumni Gym in the same week. During Loyola's magical 1985 season, Hitcho worked as the team's traveling secretary, and times were so different that Loyola and Illinois flew on the same commercial jet to Providence, R.I., for their Sweet 16 games.

Hitcho has lived through too many Loyola near-misses and mediocre basketball seasons, a trend he believes began to gradually change after the school joined the Missouri Valley Conference in 2013. He stayed away from the debate over which Loyola team was better, the 1985 group led by Alfredrick Hughes or the 2018 bunch of selfless overachievers.

"Different era," Hitcho said. "We were Chicago's team then with Alfredrick and so many players and coaches from Chicago. Not only has the city embraced us this year but as a Cinderella, we're probably a national team now. Everything is a bigger deal."

Even the humble 41-year servant of the Loyola athletic department has lost his anonymity, no matter how hard he tries to quietly blend into the background.

"I try to live the Jesuit model, being a person for others," Hitcho said. "Like St. Ignatius would say, 'Go set the world on fire.' "

Just be sure to keep Sister Jean out of harm's way. ∎

O

GUARD

DONTE INGRAM

Ingram Brings Chicago Roots to Ramblers Squad

By Shannon Ryan

As a Simeon guard, Donte Ingram watched Chicago high school stars leave the city to play college basketball.

One after another – including some of his teammates – found courts elsewhere, making it seem as if they could reach the NCAA tournament only by crossing state borders.

"Obviously, when you're a small kid, you see all those teams like Duke and North Carolina on TV," he said. "But as you get older, you start seeing (other) programs. I saw Loyola, and I saw myself fitting in."

Ingram, a 6-foot-6 senior, is one of six players on the Ramblers roster from Illinois and one of two from the Chicago Public League. He sees himself almost as the opposite of a pied piper – luring other players not away from home but persuading them by his example to seek success in Rogers Park.

"We've done a great job of just getting better every year and improving the culture and getting things better," he said. "So for kids now, they're starting to take notice, especially Chicago-area kids. I think more

city kids are going to start coming in."

A delighted coach Porter Moser slapped him encouragingly on the arm, chuckled and said, "Keep recruiting. Keep recruiting."

Ingram might be the program's best pitchman.

"I remember saying, here's a kid from the Simeon program, a Chicago kid," said Moser, who is in his seventh season. "We were Loyola of Chicago, and there was one Illinois kid on our roster. That was just nuts."

Ingram has been an integral part of the Ramblers' rise.

In the Missouri Valley Conference championship game, which earned Loyola an NCAA bid. Ingram had 18 points and eight rebounds in the final and was named the tournament's most outstanding player.

When Ingram arrived as a freshman, the program was coming off three straight losing seasons. He saw himself fitting into Moser's system and said the program had a "family" feel.

"I believed we could turn things around and be a part of something special," he said.

Ingram saw his older brother DaJuan Gouard

One of two Loyola players from the Chicago Public League, Donte Ingram was a senior leader and an indispensable player on this historic Ramblers team. (John J. Kim/Chicago Tribune)

play for a Horizon League championship in 2002 with the Ramblers.

Milton Doyle, a Public League star at Marshall who plays for the Nets' G League team, helped persuade Ingram to attend Loyola as well.

"It's like, OK, he's here and he's doing well and he's from Chicago too," Ingram said of Doyle, who graduated last year.

"It let me know I can stay in Chicago as well and leave my mark too."

* * * *

Ingram said he's "on my shoe game," owning at least 50 pairs of sneakers. His prized pair is the bright, multicolored Nikes designed last year to honor his friend and former Simeon teammate Saieed Ivey.

Ivey was fatally shot in June 2016 on his 20th birthday in Los Angeles, where he was playing basketball at a community college. Ivey's jersey number, 2, is on the top of the shoe, and the acronym "FINAO" – failure is not an option, something Ivey said frequently – is scrawled across the side.

"He was one of my first Chicago friends," Ingram said. "He was a bright person you loved being around. It's still hard. I felt like he is still with me. That was my motivation the last two seasons."

In the locker room before facing Illinois State for the MVC tournament title, Ingram cried thinking about Ivey. "I just wanted to make him proud," he said.

Ivey showed Ingram "the ropes" of navigating Simeon and Chicago. Ingram grew up in Danville, Ill., about 140 miles south of Chicago, before transferring to Simeon as a junior.

Ingram played AAU ball for Mean Streets, his family making trips to the city twice a week. Former Simeon star Jabari Parker, who was on a different AAU team, noticed Ingram on another court and he told him he should consider Simeon.

Ingram asked about moving as a freshman, but his parents weren't ready.

Don Ingram, Donte's father, said he had planned to move the family anyway because his job as a railroad engineer required so much travel to Chicago. Donte said he had "racial experiences" at Danville High School that made him want to live in a more diverse city.

As Simeon's sixth man during his junior season, Ingram helped the Wolverines to the Class 4A state championship alongside Parker.

"It was a great experience," Ingram said.

He fielded offers from Hampton and other MVC teams while drawing interest from some high-major teams. He became Loyola's first signee from Simeon since Tim Bankston in 1986.

"(It was) seeing yourself as part of the vision and the future," Ingram said. "I bought into that. I felt like I fit in great."

* * * *

Ingram was an elementary student when he visited his brother at Loyola, going to games and practices, eating in the cafeteria and sometimes having a sleepover in Gouard's dorm room.

"I wanted to show him even at young age the work ethic you've got to have," said Gouard, who played professionally in Europe and South America and now coaches at Danville Area Community College.

It's no surprise Ingram found basketball success. His dad played high school ball in New York, at community college and on base teams during 10 years in the Marine Corps. His uncle Stan Gouard is the coach at the University of Indianapolis.

As a toddler, Don Ingram placed a hoop on the end of Donte's crib and watched his son scoot to the rim and dunk a toy basketball. As he grew, his bedroom had two hoops – one affixed to the door jamb and a free-standing rim.

"He was brainwashed," Don joked.

Ingram also was dedicated to improving, especially at Loyola.

Moser said Ingram was an attractive recruit because his size and versatility made him a mismatch

Donte Ingram celebrates after beating the Kansas State Wildcats 78-62 in the Elite Eight to advance to the Final Four. Ingram had 12 points and eight rebounds in the memorable win. (John J. Kim/Chicago Tribune)

nightmare. He took a massive jump as a junior, nearly doubling his scoring average from 7.4 to 13.6.

"Every year he's gotten better," Moser said. "I think there are two years he could have gotten (the) most improved (award). I love that he was a winner."

On a team with multiple scoring options, teammates appreciate Ingram's shooting ability, consistency, timely 3-pointers (40 percent) and confidence.

"He was already a good player and he continued to get better to become a force in this league," senior guard Ben Richardson said. "He always has that big-play DNA. He's got that edge to him. That confidence oozes from him."

Ingram celebrated the Ramblers' NCAA tournament berth on the Scottrade Center court in St. Louis

with five teammates from his home state as "One Shining Moment" played. Lucas Williamson, a 6-4 freshman guard from Young, and Cameron Krutwig, a 6-9 freshman center from Jacobs in Algonquin, are future cornerstones of the program.

Ingram clutched the championship trophy and smiled.

How should Chicago fans respond to the Ramblers' success?

"Chicago needs to stand up," Ingram said. "We've been putting on for this city. We've had pride in our city. We've been taking care of business. So we've done our part."

Ingram's plan is for the city to celebrate – and for its high school players to follow in his footsteps.

GUARD

BEN RICHARDSON

Richardson Follows Teammate Custer's Advice

By Shannon Ryan

As high school teammates, Ben Richardson and Clayton Custer drove around their Kansas hometown looking for unlocked school gymnasiums they could sneak into and put up extra shots.

If someone discovered them and kicked them out – oh, well, they would just get back in the car and find another spot to play one on one. They took turns pretending to be Mario Chalmers hitting his miracle 3-pointer for Kansas in the 2008 national championship game.

So with a friendship interlaced with basketball since third grade, Custer knows better than anyone of what Richardson is capable.

"I always tell Ben he needs to shoot more every single game," Custer said of his Loyola backcourt mate.

Richardson made the biggest shots of his life in Atlanta, pushing the 11th-seeded Ramblers into the Final Four for the first time in 55 years with a 78-62 victory against No. 9 seed Kansas State.

Richardson, known for defensive tenacity, had the hottest hand on the court and the best timing a player could ask for. The senior made 6 of 7 3-pointers to score a career-high 23 points and be named the South Region's most outstanding player.

In Loyola's previous NCAA tournament games, he had scored no points against Miami, six against Tennessee and eight against Nevada. And he had strong games in all of those, thanks to his defense and passing. He had eight assists against Miami.

On a team full of scorers, Richardson has taken the second-fewest shots (137) among the seven players averaging at least 19 minutes, despite shooting a solid 46 percent from the field and 40.4 percent on 3-pointers.

He has scored at least 20 points only two other times in four seasons at Loyola. Not that he cares.

"My role is to bring energy and be a team guy," Richardson said.

Most nights, Richardson's primary task is to lock down the opponent's best player. Missouri Valley coaches and media recognized those efforts by naming Richardson the MVC defensive player of the year.

"He's always been a better defender, but he has always been able to score," Custer said. "He doesn't

Ben Richardson twirls the net after beating Kansas State to advance to the Final Four. Richardson had a huge game with 23

get as many shots. What makes him special is he doesn't care about that."

Richardson credited his big night to his teammates and to playing in a system in which coach Porter Moser stresses sharing the ball more than an elementary school teacher at recess.

"We've got so many unselfish guys, and we have so many weapons," Richardson said. "Like we've been saying, it can be anybody's night. We've shown that so far this tournament. Each one of these guys has had a big night."

At Blue Valley Northwest High School in Overland Park, Kan., the 6-foot-3 shooting guard was recruited by programs such as Indiana State and Massachusetts before selecting Loyola.

He played in four straight state championship games with back-to-back titles as a junior and senior. He was a two-time first-team all-state selection by the Kansas Basketball Coaches Association and averaged 11.4 points as a senior.

Custer recalled high school tournaments in which Richardson would explode for 20 or more points and be named the most valuable player.

"I always knew Ben was a special player," said Custer, who transferred to Loyola from Iowa State. "Everybody who's ever been around Ben knows he can play with any of these guys because he plays so hard and plays such good defense. He could play on any team in the nation. He's a coach's dream."

When the Elite Eight victory was clinched, Richardson sprinted to the sideline to cheer with Loyola fans. He pumped his arms in the air, screaming, "Let's go! Let's go!"

Standing on a ladder on the Philips Arena court, he cut down the net and whipped it over his head.

"To be living out the dream," he said, "it's something I can't even explain." ∎

Richardson is known as a tenacious defender, terrific shooter and team leader for the Ramblers. (John J. Kim/ Chicago Tribune)

CHEMISTRY MAJORS

'Mind-Blowing' Connection on Court Links Richardson, Custer

By Shannon Ryan

As fourth-graders, Ben Richardson and Clayton Custer reached the pinnacle of their youth sports careers.

At Spiece Fieldhouse in Fort Wayne, Ind., the preteen teammates won a youth basketball national championship.

"We were going out on a national stage and beating a lot of really good teams," Custer recalled. "Those were some of the coolest moments."

Sound familiar?

Loyola teammates Richardson and Custer have been repeating that success since they were around 9. They won another national championship as sixth-graders for the Overland Park Huskies. At Blue Valley Northwest High School, they went 94-6 and won two Kansas state championships.

They topped all of those experiences together Thursday evening when they helped No. 11 seed Loyola upset No. 6 Miami in the NCAA tournament, propelling them to a second-round matchup against No. 3 Tennessee.

"Every time me and Ben have played together our whole lives, we've been on winning teams," Custer said.

They were in the same first-grade class, lived a mile from each other and began playing basketball together as third-graders.

When Richardson found Custer in the corner against Miami for a game-tying 3-pointer with 1 minute, 12 seconds to play, it was the greatest pass and shot combination of their lives.

But it was nothing new.

"We had a big game for a conference championship, and it came down to the wire," said Ed Fritz, their high school coach. "Clay had the ball in his hands for the last shot, he drove, Ben came over to help. He found Ben for the layup and we won. He got fouled and (made the free throw) and we won by three points. They just have an innate ability with each other."

Fritz and Richardson's dad coached their youth team that won those national championships. Richardson credits Fritz's intensity with them – even as youngsters – for their tenacity.

Fritz, who has coached Blue Valley Northwest for 16 years, got in his car Wednesday night and drove nine hours to Dallas to catch Thursday's game. "I didn't even bring clothes," he said.

The duo told him after the game, "We played like we did when we played for you."

Overland Park, a suburb of Kansas City, is celebrating another state title Blue Valley Northwest won last weekend and is giddy about Loyola's run.

Ramblers teammates joke that Custer, a redshirt junior, and Richardson, a senior, have some kind of telekinetic connection on the court.

"They do everything together," guard Marques Townes said. "They're like brothers. They should be brothers, actually. The connection they have on the court is amazing. Being out there with them and how they find each other on the court is just mind-blowing to me."

Custer and Richardson combine for 8.2 assists per game – many to each other.

"I've had so many times people come up to me and say, 'Wow, how did you know Clay was going to be there?' " Richardson said. " 'How he did he know you were going to come behind that screen and he

Clayton Custer (left) and Ben Richardson (right) have been winning games as teammates for much of their lives, a trend that only continued on this unforgettable Loyola team. (John J. Kim/Chicago Tribune)

was going to find you like that?' It's just chemistry we've worked on countless hours in the gym."

They parted ways initially for college as Custer went to Iowa State and Richardson headed for Rogers Park. Custer played in only 12 games as a freshman with limited minutes and decided to find a program where he could make a more significant impact.

Before he even received his release from Iowa State, Custer confided in Richardson, who immediately started recruiting him.

"He was like, 'You have to come on a visit,'" Custer said. "He basically said even if you don't like Loyola, just come visit and we'll have a great time."

Coach Porter Moser saw Custer play in high school when he recruited Richardson. When Custer got his release, "it was game on," Moser said. "It was the foot on the gas pedal."

Custer committed to Loyola on that visit.

Three years later, Custer is the Missouri Valley Conference player of the year and Richardson the league's defensive player of the year.

After the Ramblers won the MVC tournament, the duo walked beside each other from the court to a media interview room. They told each other: "Man, can you believe this? We've won since we were in third grade."

Moser watched the scene unfold with pride.

"It was the most genuine, little-kid moment of two grown guys just sharing it," he said.

Richardson marveled at the experiences he and Custer have enjoyed together.

"There's no way for it to set in now," he said. "We've had countless lifelong memories already. This will go at the top of the list, I think. We're not done yet. We want to make some more good ones." ∎

13

GUARD

CLAYTON CUSTER

Porter Moser 'Went Out of His Way' to Land Clayton Custer

By Shannon Ryan

Loyola coach Porter Moser had a little more than 24 hours to land his targeted point guard. Clayton Custer had been granted his request for a release of scholarship from Iowa State shortly before a window closed when the NCAA permits college coaches to contact recruits. Moser had to work fast.

He drove to Ames, Iowa, to meet with Custer for lunch at the most famous restaurant in the college town.

"I saw the passion in his eyes," Custer said. "I instantly started believing in him."

Moser then drove nearly four hours south in his rental car to Overland Park, Kan., to talk to Custer's parents, Galen and Terri, in the family's suburban Kansas City living room.

"He really went out of his way to get Clayton," Terri Custer said.

The miles paid off.

Custer bumped Loyola to the top of his list of potential transfer destinations, pushing back his planned visits to Creighton and Wichita State. On his official visit in April 2015 to Loyola, where his best friend and high school teammate Ben Richardson played, he was sold and committed while on campus.

"When you decide to transfer it's a scary thing," Custer said. "You don't know who's going to give you an opportunity. You don't know if you're going to get another opportunity. I don't think I could have picked a better place."

Wearing his maroon No. 13 Loyola jersey talking to reporters on the eve of the Final Four, a retrospective look shows that everything turned out splendidly for Custer. The 6-foot-1 redshirt junior, who sat out the 2015-16 season after transferring, was named the Missouri Valley Conference player of the year after guiding the No. 11 Ramblers through a magical season.

Custer might be recognized mostly for his game-winning shot in the closing seconds of a second-round victory against Tennessee. But he has been more vital for his steady play and leadership than for dramatic plays, averaging 13.2 points and 4.2 assists per game while shooting 52.7 percent from the field.

Clayton Custer gestures after making a 3-pointer in Loyola's 64-62 win over Miami in the first round of the NCAA Tournament. Custer hit four 3-pointers in the game on his way to 14 points. (John J. Kim/Chicago Tribune)

"He's like our general," Loyola forward Aundre Jackson said.

Loyola especially understood how Custer made the offense "click" when his left ankle injury caused him to miss five games during the season. The Ramblers (32-5) went 2-3 in that stretch, collecting the majority of their few losses.

"Clay is a well-rounded, unselfish player," Richardson said. "He can run our offense and get things going like nobody else. He's unique in the way that he knows how to make plays for others, and he also can go get a shot for himself. He really infuses the rest of us with a ton of confidence."

Custer's journey to the Final Four didn't start in Rogers Park's Gentile Arena or even at Iowa State.

It started back in Overland Park, Kan., where a young Custer would tag along to his 10-years older brother Brandon's games. Custer's first choice for play was basketball. He spent so much time dribbling at playgrounds, his mom realized when he was about 5 he hadn't learned how to swing on the playground.

Ed Fritz, Custer's youth coach and Blue Valley Northwest High School coach, noticed early how Custer was driven to "perfectionism."

By the time Custer earned his driver's license, Fritz left the key to the high school gym under his welcome mat for Custer, who would return it after hours of shooting around on his own.

Fritz recalled a game when Iowa State lost to Kansas while Custer was in high school. He had committed to Iowa State as a sophomore and watching the loss of his future program motivated him. He called Fritz, luring him out of his home in a snowstorm to meet him at the gym to work him out.

"He wanted to make sure the same thing wouldn't happen to him," he said.

Then there was the New Year's Eve – either in 2008 or 2009, Fritz said – when Custer gathered his middle school teammates at the gym to ring in another year playing basketball at midnight. They played until about 2 a.m.

"There was no place he would rather be," Fritz said.

Custer won two state championships alongside Richardson, now a Loyola senior backcourt mate to Custer. Fritz raves about Custer's passing, hand-eye coordination, ability to change speeds while dribbling, his ambidextrous shooting and his pull-up jumper. But mostly, he credits Custer's work ethic.

"He had a lot of drive and a lot of determination you don't see in someone that young," Fritz said. "If he had a bad game, he worked twice as hard to make sure it didn't happen again."

He received offers from Big 12 schools such as Oklahoma State and Kansas State. He had grown up a Kansas fan, his father's alma mater, and attended camps at Allen Fieldhouse. Jayhawks coach Bill Self – a potential national championship opponent for Loyola – approached him after one game at a camp.

"He came up and said, 'Clay, you're good enough to play at KU,'" Custer recalled. "We just are too loaded at guard right now. It wouldn't make sense.' I respect him 100 percent."

At Iowa State, playing under current Bulls coach Fred Hoiberg, Custer averaged only 5.8 minutes and 1.1 points per game as a freshman. After being a pivotal player in every program he played in since third grade, sitting on the bench seemed futile.

Custer was the leading scorer for Loyola during the 2017-2018 season and was voted the Missouri Valley Conference Player of the Year. (John J. Kim/Chicago Tribune)

"It was a low point in his basketball life for sure," Terri Custer said. "You spend all that time trying to find the right fit. It's very hard."

Custer called his decision to leave "emotional."

Richardson convinced Custer to give Loyola a chance. And Moser was aggressive in his pursuit, telling the Custer family he halted all other recruiting until he got a "yes" from Custer. He devoted his final day of recruiting in that open period to chasing Custer.

"I pretty much knew I was in because Ben was like, 'Game on,'" Moser said. "(I thought,) 'All right. We're getting him.'"

After punching a ticket to the Final Four with a victory against Kansas State, Moser saw Custer's parents later that night at the team hotel in Atlanta.

"I had Galen and Terri (and Clayton), all three in a bear hug back at the hotel," Moser said. "I said, 'That was the best living room visit I ever did on a one-day (trip).'"

Reflecting on his journey that has met its destination in San Antonio, Custer can take comfort in his decisions that led him to Loyola.

"He's in the Final Four," Terri Custer said. "It looks like a pretty good thing." ■

BAND OF WOLVES

Loyola's Pep Band Brings the Spirit

By HOWARD REICH

If you thought the Loyola Ramblers are good at what they do, you should check out the Band of Wolves.

That's the school's pep band, which plays all the team's home games and has been on the road quite a bit the past few weeks, as the Ramblers ascended to the NCAA Tournament's Final Four.

This week, when the rest of the Loyola student body was doing homework or playing video games or otherwise occupying itself, the Band of Wolves was thundering in the corridors of the Gentile Arena, where the team has triumphed this season. The student musicians couldn't get onto the actual court, because a TV news crew had taken over the place, now that Loyola basketball has become a national phenomenon.

So Frederick "Rick" Lowe, director of ensembles at Loyola University Chicago and leader of the Band of Wolves, conducted his young musicians out in the hallways for a last rehearsal before they head to San Antonio for the Final Four. At one point during practice, a building security alarm went off, producing a piercing shriek that cried out for at least 15 minutes without stop.

Undaunted, the musicians and their leader simply kept rehearsing, though perhaps even more loudly than usual.

"We need to work on memorization, because we're faking it," Lowe told the students.

The Loyola pep band practices in San Antonio before the Ramblers' historic Final Four appearance. (Brian Cassella/ Chicago Tribune)

"What I've been noticing about the fight song – and the songs in general – is we get so excited, we're running out of breath," added Lowe, who then began singing long, lovely, legato tones, by way of demonstration.

"You've got to sustain notes!"

Lest anyone think that the pep band simply makes noise while the rest of the stadium is yelling, it's worth noting that these students must master complex arrangements of more than two dozen stylistically far-reaching pieces. From the feel-good spirit of Neil Diamond's "Sweet Caroline" to the surging energy of Survivor's "Eye of the Tiger" to the anthemlike refrain of Chicago's "25 or 6 to 4," the young musicians have to be able to hit in unison an instant after Lowe gives the cue.

That means he'll flash some hand signals, then wave the downbeat. So when Lowe puts up two fingers on each hand, that signifies "22," which instantly tells the students they're about to launch into song No. 22: "Sweet Caroline."

"We have a couple of 'engagement songs' that go over really well, and 'Sweet Caroline' is one of those," said senior Christian Pratt, a clarinetist and double major in biology and music, just before the rehearsal.

"The crowd will sing along on the bom-bom-bom part.

"And we have a couple of Chicago-y tunes that everyone likes: 'Sweet Home Chicago,' 'I Can't Turn You Loose' – a Blues Brothers tune (by Otis Redding) – and '25 or 6 to 4.'"

But the band gets a little more contemporary, too, sometimes offering Bruno Mars' "Runaway Baby" and Pitbull's "Fireball."

What makes all of this challenging is that only about 15 percent of the band members are music majors, according to Lowe's estimate. The rest come from various academic disciplines and backgrounds, making for a motley crew.

"I might have two percussionists, two horns and no one on bass," explains Lowe. "How am I going to make this work?

"The second major challenge is choosing the right repertoire. Because we have such a mix of (music) majors and nonmajors, there's a really broad range of experience and talent. So trying to find pieces that can push the level up, but also are still playable, is a constant journey."

The students receive no course credit but must rehearse and perform steadily. In the fall, they "cram in three or four rehearsals" during Band Week, said Lowe, then practice weekly after that. Once the season gets underway in mid-November, they play two to three games a week.

Why do they do it?

"I just finished applying to law school ... it's a good stress reliever," said senior Zachary Manzella, a drummer and political science major. "You go out and hit something – in a musical fashion, of course."

For senior Katie Spear, a mellophone player who majors in environmental science and film and digital media, playing in the Band of Wolves has been a game-changer (the team is named for Loyola's mascot, the wolf).

"Marian was very intense," said Spear, who played in the Marian Catholic High School marching band, in Chicago Heights, one of the most celebrated such ensembles in the country. "There was lots of practice.

"I came here," to Loyola, added Spear, "and I didn't have that. And I was feeling a bit confused. I was thinking of transferring.

"Pep band stopped me from deciding to transfer."

No one, though, expected what has happened this year.

"It's crazy," said clarinetist Pratt. "We never thought it would go on this long. Usually we're done the first week in March."

Said drummer Manzella, "It's something I've never experienced in my time here. When I got here my freshman year, the success of the team just started. Since then, the band has grown along with the basketball program."

Of course, there have been stresses along the way.

Jared Jurss, a junior and bioinformatics major, acknowledged that his enormous Sousaphone "gets

Loyola pep band director Rick Lowe leads his students in a final rehearsal at Gentile Arena before making the trip to support the Ramblers in the Final Four. (Chris Sweda/Chicago Tribune)

heavy after a while." Sophomore Courtney Carmack, a biology major with an ecology emphasis, nodded in agreement as she produced a mighty tone on her own Sousaphone.

"There's been a lot of missing school, so I'm lucky it's my senior spring," said Spear. "I don't regret missing some classes. It's been insane – we've never had this kind of school spirit before."

That was obvious throughout the rehearsal.

"I've heard the Michigan coach is a big fan of funk music, so I want to beat them to the punch," Lowe told the students, referencing the Michigan team that Loyola will play Saturday in San Antonio.

With that, Lowe signaled "45," meaning Parliament-Funkadelic's "Give Up the Funk (Tear the Roof Off the Sucker)" – which the band proceeded to do.

Maybe that's what set off the security alarm.

The students also punched their way through the school's fight song, "Hail Loyola," and, at evening's end, Lowe led a magisterial performance of "Hail to You, Loyola," the regal, choralelike alma mater.

All of which made one wonder what will happen when the Final Four is over and reality sets back in.

Until now, "A lot of people weren't aware that you could come to Loyola and study music," said Lowe, who hopes that the pep band's performances on national TV and all the other media exposure will heighten the profile of Loyola's music program.

"You cannot buy press like this," he added.

Finally, it was time to wind down.

"Good playing tonight," Lowe told the students.

"When we're getting on the plane, I want us to take (music) books with us, so we can look at them."

Even up in the air, the work will continue. ∎

GUARD

MARQUES TOWNES

Hoops Turns Out to be Right Choice for Loyola's Townes

By Shannon Ryan

Marques Townes wrestled with the decision – almost too long. Football or basketball?

The Edison, N.J., native was the rare modern athlete who not only dedicated himself to two sports, but also excelled at both.

Power Five football programs such as Penn State, Maryland and Rutgers showed strong interest. Akron, Ball State and Syracuse offered scholarships to the outside linebacker and running back.

In basketball, Townes played at St. Joseph alongside future NBA players Karl-Anthony Towns and Wade Baldwin IV and ranked second in school history in points (1,863) behind former Duke great and Bulls guard Jay Williams.

Townes didn't know which direction would be best. So he waited. As a result, he said, some schools rescinded their basketball scholarship offers as they filled their recruiting slots.

"It was a frustrating process because I didn't know what I wanted to do," said Townes, now a junior guard at Loyola. "I got to the point, I've got to sit down and think about what I've got to do. I talked to my dad,

my mom, my AAU coach. I felt like it was my decision at the end of the day. My heart was with basketball, and I couldn't give up that passion."

He signed in April of his senior year with Fairleigh Dickinson, a Northeast Conference program not far from home, and he started every game as a sophomore, averaging 11.5 points as the Knights reached the 2016 NCAA tournament, losing a First Four game to Florida Gulf Coast. But after that season he decided to transfer.

Despite having never been to Chicago or having heard of Loyola, he visited the campus and ultimately transferred there.

Now, after sitting out last season because of NCAA transfer rules, Townes is back in the NCAA tournament with the 11th-seeded Ramblers.

His football background isn't irrelevant to his success.

"We call him a bulldozer," Loyola forward Aundre Jackson said. "He's always full speed."

"We call him a big guard," freshman guard Lucas Williamson said.

Townes' physical play is part of what attracted Loyola to the 6-foot-4, 210-pound guard when it

Marques Townes reacts after making a basket in Loyola's win over Miami in the first round of the NCAA tournament. Townes had seven points in the upset victory. (John J. Kim/ Chicago Tribune)

worked to land him after his decision to transfer.

"I saw he could get to the basket," said assistant coach Bryan Mullins, who recruited Townes. "The (Missouri) Valley is such a physical conference. His body was ready to make an impact right away. That impressed us.

"He's got a good change of speed. He's a guard who can get to the basket and finish. He gave us a different look than we've had in the past. In transition he's great. He can get downhill so easily." Townes initially quit football when he got to high school to focus on basketball. He missed the sport watching from the stands, and St. Joseph football coach Casey Ransone urged him to play his senior season.

"He was just such a rare athlete," Ransone said. "It was my personal opinion if he had stayed with football, he would have become an NFL linebacker."

Ransone referred to basketball players who turned into NFL stars, such as Tony Gonzalez, Julius Peppers and Antonio Gates, to make his point about how Townes' toughness and athleticism could have translated to football.

Most college football programs wanted Townes to enroll in prep school for a year to develop further. Ransone said Townes easily could have added muscle to become a 230-pound linebacker.

He tried to tell Townes he would have more opportunities in football. Townes could have a shot at the NBA but almost certainly would find a role on an overseas basketball team.

"He had so much invested in basketball," Ransone said. "It was tough. I told him his football ceiling is higher. It would have (gone) further in the end. But I see how it's worked out. In the end he's made the right decision."

Even after Townes announced his transfer from Fairleigh Dickinson, Ransone said Syracuse football coaches called him wondering if Townes had any interest in returning to the gridiron.

"I was like, 'No, I'm not coming back,'" Townes said. "I just wanted to play basketball."

Townes has no regrets.

"Look where we are now," he said. ∎

Townes' background in football has helped make him one of the most physical and athletic players on the Ramblers. (John J. Kim/ Chicago Tribune)

BEST FOOT FORWARD

Loyola Players Pick Their Sneakers Carefully

BY SHANNON RYAN

A few days before the Sweet 16, Loyola guard Marques Townes was texting with an NBA player who had competed in the Final Four.

He could have asked for any advice at all, but the conversation with Karl Anthony-Towns, a former Kentucky star, was all about shoes.

"He was like, 'Man, just wear the most comfortable shoes,'" said Townes, who played with Towns in high school in New Jersey. "'It's no fashion show. Just be comfortable out there; be you.'"

Townes has been donning his comfy, salmon-colored "Hollywood LeBron" pair throughout the tournament since that talk. And Loyola has continued to roll all the way to the Final Four, where the No. 11 seed will face Michigan on Saturday in San Antonio's Alamodome.

Before college basketball players prepare for the most significant games of their lives in the NCAA tournament, they pour over scouting reports, absorb last-minute details from coaches, work on their shot – and, yes, they spend an awful lot of time deciding what to wear on their feet.

The NFL fines players for wearing shoes that differentiate them from teammates. College football programs are uniform in footwear too – all black or all white cleats.

Ben Richardson inspects teammate Marques Townes' favored kicks. Townes sported the salmon pink pair throughout Loyola's NCAA Tournament run. (John J. Kim/Chicago Tribune)

"I like to switch it up and give different looks out there." – Donte Ingram

But NBA players are free to express themselves – and promote their own brands. College basketball players are eager to emulate them with sneakers of the stars, and as long as they wear the brand that sponsors their team, college players' style preference can be whatever they wish.

"I'm a sneaker-head, so I like to make sure I'm on my A-game with that," said Loyola senior Donte Ingram, who owns about 50 pairs of basketball shoes.

His prized pair is bright, multicolored "Nike Hyperdunk Low Chicago" designed last year to honor his friend and former Simeon teammate Saieed Ivey, who was shot fatally in June 2016. The shoes feature Ivey's jersey number, 2, and the acronym "FINAO" – failure is not an option – which Ivey said frequently.

But in Saturday's Final Four game against Michigan, Ingram will wear white Aunt Pearl KDs.

"I like to switch it up and give different looks out there," he said.

Other players select their shoes for function. Some wear the same pair until they are near decay.

"They're nasty," Michigan forward Moe Wagner said, looking down at his black, boat-sized Jordan 11s. "I'll be so happy when the season is over, so I can throw them away. Or I'll keep them as a memory. They won't make it long."

Wagner wears them because they allow his right ankle brace to fit inside. But his teammates rib him for his old-school style.

"They're giving me a lot of – I'm not going to say the s-word – a lot of stuff for wearing these retros," Wagner said.

Loyola freshman Lucas Williamson wore his PG 1 pair last season at Whitney Young all the way until the NCAA tournament before upgrading to a pair of PG 2s. He wears them because he hopes to emulate Paul George's play.

"I'm going to stick with these," Williamson said.

Michigan senior guard Muhammad-Ali Abdur-Rahkman might be the hardest player to miss on the court – and not only because of his shot. They don't exactly match his maize-and-blue uniform, but his hot pink Air Jordan XXXII shoes make him the flashiest player on the court.

He wore them last season for a game promoting breast cancer awareness, and then after Michigan's plane skidded off the runway before the 2017 Big Ten tournament they were the only pair Abdur-Rahkman had available. He shot well and has laced them back up this season.

"I just feel I have a certain swag 'bout me when I wear them," he said.

Don't they all? ∎

Guard Donte Ingram enjoys showcasing a variety of looks with his on-court footwear. (John J. Kim/Chicago Tribune)

24

FORWARD

AUNDRE JACKSON

The Struggle is Part of the Story

By Shannon Ryan

Aundre Jackson had just finished his junior-college career with a loss in the 2016 national semifinals when a coach from a school he had never heard of stopped by the team hotel in Hutchinson, Kan., to make a recruiting pitch.

Jackson was still sulking about McLennan Community College's 96-91 loss, in which he had scored 25 points, when Loyola's Porter Moser encouraged him to look to the future.

"We lost, so I was emotional," Jackson recalled. "But (Moser and I) just clicked. He just talked about: 'This is your next step. Juco is behind you.' He talked about the culture at Loyola. It was a perfect fit."

Jackson, now a senior, has proved to be an important cog in a Loyola team whose system depends on every part.

The 6-foot-5, 230-pound forward has delivered on the mismatch abilities that drew Moser to check him out in that juco tournament. A spark off the bench, Jackson averages 10.9 points and shoots 57.6 percent from the field.

Competing Thursday for 11th-seeded Loyola (28-5) against No. 6 seed Miami (22-9) in the NCAA tournament in Dallas -- near his hometown of Fort Worth -- reminds Jackson why he chose these words last summer to be tattooed on the inside of his left forearm:

"The struggle is part of the story."

Coming out of Kennedale High School, about 20 minutes southeast of Fort Worth, Jackson fielded offers from Division II and Division III programs.

"I thought I was better," he said. "People advised me, 'Most people out of juco don't make it.' I had a plan. I had a vision. It wasn't a hard decision. I really wanted this. I really wanted to be a Division I athlete."

At McLennan in Waco, Texas, Jackson ranked fourth nationally as a sophomore by shooting nearly 65 percent from the field and averaged 15 points and seven rebounds.

"As we were making our way, building this team, it was hard to get these 6-9 athletes with high rankings," Moser said. "Sometimes you sign a kid (who's) 6-8, 6-9 because your boosters and everyone (are) saying you've got to have some size.

"I didn't really care about that. Aundre is a get-it-done guy. I've made a living off undersized guys. I like

Aundre Jackson had 12 points in the win against Miami, the first NCAA Tournament game for the Ramblers since 1985. (John J. Kim/ Chicago Tribune)

guys who play bigger than they are, not smaller than they are. And Aundre is a guy who plays bigger than he is."

Jackson said his McLennan experience made him a better, tougher player.

"Juco is a grind," he said. "Everybody that goes to juco, they want it. Every game, they're going to try to go for your neck. You have to be on top of your game and be ready for a battle every game. It just made me hungrier. You can't take a day off or settle."

It's no surprise Jackson won a perfect attendance award in high school. He shows up every game for Loyola too.

He has shot at least 50 percent from the field in 24 games. After being named Missouri Valley Conference sixth man of the year last season, Jackson moved into a starting role for the first 13 games this season before Moser moved him back to the bench when Ben Richardson returned from injury.

His minutes dipped only slightly, and his production remained steady.

"He means a lot to this team," senior wing Donte Ingram said. "He's really a starter if you ask me. He's a mismatch nightmare. He does a great job scoring and bringing energy off the bench."

As soon as Jackson heard Loyola's name called during TBS' Selection Sunday show, he called his mom.

"He was like, 'Mama, I'm coming to Dallas,'" LaTrisha Jackson said. "I was so happy I could have cried."

Jackson has been bragging to his teammates about Texas' warm weather and Southern hospitality. When the Ramblers tip off in their first NCAA tournament game in 33 years, he will spot family, friends, former coaches and teammates in the American Airlines Center stands.

Jackson has been reflecting on his journey and appreciating reaching his sport's biggest stage.

"It's a great feeling," he said. ∎

Jackson brings an offensive spark off the bench and is considered an honorary sixth member of the starting lineup. (John J. Kim/ Chicago Tribune)

25

CENTER

CAMERON KRUTWIG

Big Man on Campus

BY SHANNON RYAN

Late one night, after snipping down nets and wading through confetti, Loyola freshman Cameron Krutwig met three of his high school buddies in his Atlanta hotel room when an idea struck.

The giddy teenagers scurried to the closest Dairy Queen for celebratory Blizzards shortly before closing time at about 11 p.m., toasting their best friend's ride to the Final Four.

"I don't get to spend time with those guys that much anymore," Krutwig said of his former teammates at Jacobs High School in Algonquin. "We get windows. We just wanted to be with each other and spend some time catching up. I love those guys."

The Final Four storyline about the conspicuous absence of freshmen stars conveniently overlooks Krutwig.

The 19-year-old who became a starter just three games into his college career hardly resembles a freshman – besides his boyish grin, Will Ferrell impersonations and ironically off-key Christmas carol singing group (we'll get to that later).

Far from the one-and-done type of youngster we're accustomed to seeing sparkle on this stage, Krutwig is a key player for the No. 11 seeded Ramblers who will take on No. 3 seed Michigan in San Antonio in their first Final Four since 1963's national championship team.

Few college players are like him -- a traditional big man at 6-foot-9 and 260 pounds who is also a deft passer.

Averaging 10.3 points, 6.1 rebounds and 1.8 assists per game, he's been reliable and productive. His soft touch from the post supplied seven assists against UIC in the regular season, and he's had eight other games with at least three assists, including a seven-point, four-assist performance against towering Tennessee in a second-round victory.

"It's a pressure release sometimes when guys are pressuring me or any of us at the top," point guard Clayton Custer said. "If he flashes to the elbow, we throw it to him there and then we can cut off him and he can make passes off of it. He's a playmaker as a

Cameron Krutwig has played beyond his years as a freshman, averaging 10.3 points, 6.1 rebounds and 1.8 assists per game.

five-man, which is amazing."

While his low-post game is a throwback and his passing skills are rare for any center, Krutwig's ability to play down low as a freshman without fouling might be his most impressive feat. He has not fouled out once this season while averaging 23.6 minutes per game, recording four fouls only twice.

Assistant coach Matt Gordon said: "It starts with him being one of the smartest kids I've ever coached."

Krutwig follows coach Porter Moser's "through you to the rim" and "reach for the lights" mantras for defending the post. He will be challenged Saturday when the Ramblers face Michigan's 6-11 versatile center Moe Wagner, who averages 14.3 points and 6.9 rebounds while putting up four 3-pointers per game.

"Sometimes bigs get in foul trouble because they're trying to block so many shots," Moser said. "Coach (Rick) Majerus had a great line: Know who you are. And Cam knows who he is. He's not a shot blocker. He's got to rotate and be big, rotate through the rim. He's got to take some charges."

Senior Ben Richardson called Krutwig the most vocal player on the team as his teammates and coach nodded.

Those who knew him at Jacobs, where a good luck message for Krutwig is displayed on the announcement board in front of the school, said he's always been like that. Outgoing, down to earth, and fitting in with ease.

His "goofball" mentality, as Custer put it, ingratiates him with his teammates as it did at Jacobs, where he led the Eagles to a 30-2 record and a sectional championship as a senior.

As high school sophomores, he and five friends formed the "Six Cheersmen," a mock vocal group specializing in dog-howl-inducing renditions of holiday carols. They've produced an album – made with a phone sitting on a chair in a basement – each of the last

three years. Krutwig proudly has the music pinned to the top of his Twitter page.

Krutwig called their version of "Silent Night" "ear-scratching."

"None of us would you say is musically talented," said his friend and Six Cheersman member Cooper Schwartz. "But we sure are passionate."

Said Krutwig: "We're a hometown group. We're born and raised in Algonquin, Illinois. People will text us: 'This is so bad.' ... Honestly, we're not any good. But it's just fun. We can be dumb and stupid and laugh with each other."

Final Four fame isn't getting to Krutwig, Schwartz said. "I think he'll remain humble, a Cheersman for life."

Krutwig grew up shadowing his brother Conrad, eight years older and also a star at Jacobs who played at South Dakota and Wisconsin-Parkside. "When he was little, we had some driveway battles," Cameron Krutwig said. "I busted him pretty good."

Krutwig learned early what it was like to be thrust into a spotlight. At Jacobs, he entered the starting lineup about 10 games into his freshman season. Double- and triple-teams were common.

Throughout his career, Jacobs coach Jimmy Roberts said, Krutwig performed his best in the biggest games. Roberts pointed to a sectional final against Larkin when the center was one assist away from a quadruple double (20 points, 23 rebounds, 11 blocks and nine assists).

Krutwig won three regional championships at Jacobs and holds nine team records.

When Roberts watched the Sweet 16 and Elite Eight victories at Philips Arena, he received texts from friends pointing out how recruiters missed out on Krutwig. He fielded about 30 mostly mid-major scholarship offers, but none from DePaul or the Big Ten.

"The comments were the same across the board:

Krutwig brings production on the court and a "goofball" mentality off the court, endearing him to his teammates early in his Loyola career. (John J. Kim/ Chicago Tribune)

'Just not tall enough. We're concerned about him physically. We're concerned about ball screens. Can he run up and down the floor?' "Roberts said. "It's kind of funny now."

Krutwig, who lost 30 pounds before this season, said he was in love with Loyola anyway, sensing how well he would fit in with a team that shared the ball. An old soul who loves Larry Bird and Mark Price in basketball and the Beach Boys and Temptations in music, he savors his traditional role.

Heading into the Final Four, the biggest basketball moment of his young life, Krutwig said he feels loose.

"I don't feel any pressure," he said. "I'm a freshman. I'm supposed to be not that good, so It's not as much pressure."

He's just having fun. ∎

YEARS IN THE MAKING

The Two Key Decisions that Helped Loyola Reach the Final Four

BY DAVID HAUGH • MARCH 27, 2018

E tch March 24, 2018 into the lore of Loyola basketball. But two other dates mean almost as much as the one that will mark the school making its first Final Four in 55 years.

Without the milestones that preceded Loyola's historic Elite 8 victory over Kansas State, Porter Moser might be flying commercial to San Antonio this week to attend a coaches convention rather than coach an NCAA semifinal.

The first is April 5, 2011, the day Loyola named Moser its new basketball coach.

The second is July 1, 2013, the moment Loyola officially joined the Missouri Valley Conference.

Both moves qualified as quantum leaps of faith, decisions that required vision not every athletic director possesses when plotting a program's future. When DePaul and Illinoisfans, for instance, lament how Loyola has surpassed them in the state of Illinois, they can trace their respective problems back to strategic mistakes the Ramblers simply didn't make at similarly critical junctures. Loyola's hunches paid off while the guesses made by administrators at DePaul and Illinois have looked anything but educated.

Former Loyola athletic director Grace Calhoun presided over both big decisions that positioned the Ramblers for long-term success.

In 2013, Loyola joined the Missouri Valley Conference. In 2018, the MVC championship represented just the beginning of their extraordinary accomplishments. (Nancy Stone/Chicago Tribune)

At the 2011 press conference introducing Moser, Calhoun vowed the energetic new Loyola coach would "bring unparalleled integrity, passion and energy to the men's basketball program." Cynics in the audience could have been forgiven for rolling their eyes: Moser, then a St. Louis assistant, had gone 51-67 over four seasons at his previous head-coaching stop at Illinois State. Yet Calhoun was sold by the same sincerity, passion and meticulousness that makes Moser the most compelling Final Four coach this season. The risk was rewarded.

Two years after Moser's hiring, in 2013, Calhoun announced a partnership with the Missouri Valley Conference that "will enhance our visibility and have a positive impact on the experience of our student-athletes." The way Loyola has shot from relative obscurity to prosperity since winning the MVC tournament earlier this month fulfilled Calhoun's pledge. The step up from the Horizon League improved the caliber of recruit interested in Loyola, especially in Chicago and in-state, as well as access to the NCAA tournament given the national respect shown the MVC.

Wichita State leaving the league this year indeed created a clearer path to the NCAA tournament – as critics have pointed out, as if to diminish the achievement – but Loyola winning four March Madness games disproved any doubts about their legitimacy. Conference realignment happens often in college sports but seldom do teams take advantage to the extent Loyola has.

Calhoun, now the athletic director at Penn, declined a Tribune request for an interview about her role in Loyola's rise because "she wants to keep the focus on the Loyola student-athletes, coaches, administrators and community instead of her," a spokesman said. "But she is really excited for Loyola, Porter and the entire university community on making the Final Four."

Meanwhile, DePaul and Illinois whiffed when faced with similar chances to hit administrative home runs.

So much about DePaul basketball warrants scrutiny since the school joined the Big East before the 2005-2006 season. The steady demise of the Blue Demons raises questions whether that was the right move for the men's basketball program, which once enjoyed a tradition that appealed to the Big East. Since joining the conference, DePaul has won just 35 percent of its games (143-265) and finished 10th or lower in the league standings 10 times, never higher than seventh.

Does DePaul know what it is? Or what it isn't? You wonder how many folks on the Lincoln Park campus long for the Conference USA days when DePaul posted three straight 20-win seasons from 2002-2005 in a league more compatible for its talent level. DePaul plays in a first-class facility at Wintrust Arena but the product fails to compare to what's on display at Gentile Arena.

Athletic director Jean Lenti Ponsetto had a chance to make her own bold hire in 2015 after firing Oliver Purnell – like Calhoun did with Moser – but settled for the familiarity of nice guy Dave Leitao, who has been unable to turn things around in three seasons. If Loyola's Final Four run doesn't force the DePaul hierarchy to hold Lenti Ponsetto more accountable immediately – Leitao is her third unsuccessful coaching hire since joining the Big East – nothing will.

Illinois believes it found the right man in coach Brad Underwood, who showed promise in his first season. Problem is, organizational missteps hiring Underwood's predecessor, John Groce, put Illinois in position to be passed by Loyola. Groce accepted former Illinois athletic director Mike Thomas' job offer in late March 2012 only after at least five other candidates passed on pursuing it. It was the corporate definition of settling.

At the time, Groce was a 40-year-old head coach with a 34-30 record in the Mid-American Conference.

Clayton Custer signs autographs as fans welcome the Ramblers back to campus after the team advanced to the Sweet 16 of the NCAA Tournament. (Brian Cassella/ Chicago Tribune)

In five seasons at Illinois, Groce maintained mediocrity, going 95-75 with a 39-53 Big Ten record and only one NCAA appearance. Illinois never showed the patience in Groce that Loyola did in Moser, who struggled early, but it was much less apparent why the Illini should. Nothing special ever stood out about Groce's program.

The right man for the job makes it more immediately obvious he is. The way Moser did with Calhoun and Steve Watson, Loyola's current athletic director. The way Chris Collins did with Northwestern athletic director Jim Phillips. Execution at any level of sports begins with inspiration, winning starts with dreaming.

Loyola's inspired choices made so many dreams come true. ■

MARCH 2, 2018 · ST. LOUIS, MISSOURI

LOYOLA 54, NORTHERN IOWA 50

WON DOWN, TWO TO GO

Inspired Richardson Helps Push Ramblers Two Wins from NCAAs

BY SHANNON RYAN

Just three games into Loyola's season, captain Ben Richardson broke his left hand and needed surgery.

"You just want to break your heart when you get a senior (who is) injured," coach Porter Moser said.

Richardson's response to sitting out a month and missing 10 games defined the Ramblers' unselfish culture.

"He says to me, 'Well, maybe this will give somebody else a chance to step up and get more minutes, and then when I come back, we'll be deeper,'" Moser recalled. "I mean, who says that?"

Richardson does.

The Ramblers needed someone to step up in the Missouri Valley Conference quarterfinals against No. 9 seed Northern Iowa when MVC player of the year Clayton Custer struggled with his shot. It was Richardson who helped show off Loyola's depth with some big shots and his typical gritty defense for a 54-50 victory that kept the Ramblers' NCAA tournament hopes alive.

Top seed Loyola (26-5) advanced to face Bradley in the semifinals at the Scottrade Center. The fifth-seeded Braves beat Drake 63-61 on a last-second layup by Donte Thomas.

Richardson's four steals were vital. But it was his 3-pointer at the shot-clock buzzer with less than 7 minutes remaining that provided a boost and a 40-37 edge for the Ramblers, who had trailed by six.

"We have a lot of weapons on this team," said Richardson, who finished with nine points and six assists. "Any guy can go make that big play. At that point in the game, I had to take it."

Loyola had been known for its shooting during its MVC championship regular season. The Ramblers entered Friday ranked second nationally at 51.4 percent.

But they had to find a different way to beat the Panthers, who were fourth nationally in holding opponents to 62.9 points a game.

"It was gritty. It was tough. It was ugly at times," Moser said.

Loyola made only one of its first 10 shots. Custer, who injured an ankle Friday, shot 1 of 7 from the field, making a layup with 5:41 remaining.

"I'm telling you, he's going to make some huge plays for us here in St. Louis," Moser promised. ∎

Ramblers guard Clayton Custer goes up for a shot past Northern Iowa Panthers forward Bennett Koch during the second half of Loyola's 54-50 win. (AP Images)

MVC TOURNAMENT SEMIFINALS
MARCH 3, 2018 · ST. LOUIS, MISSOURI
LOYOLA 62, BRADLEY 54

CHASING TO THE END

Ramblers Win Ninth in a Row, Reach Tourney Final

BY SHANNON RYAN

Since Loyola took over the conference lead in the middle of the Missouri Valley season, coach Porter Moser has scoffed at the idea of the Ramblers being a targeted team.

There's no doubt the Ramblers have been wearing a bull's-eye, but Moser didn't want his players thinking of themselves as being chased. They were going on an unending journey, the way Moser told it.

"All the questions I was getting were about, 'What's it feel like now (that) everyone's chasing you?' And I just was like, we're chasing,'" Moser said. "We don't have any championship banners in the Missouri Valley. We don't have anything. Being in first place in the middle of (the season) wasn't what our finish line was."

He told the players their new motto: "No finish line."

Loyola's run reached the MVC tournament championship game after a 62-54 semifinal victory over Bradley at Scottrade Center. The Ramblers will face Illinois State in the title game with a guaranteed trip to the NCAA tournament on the line.

No matter how the Ramblers want to define it, it would be a rare milestone for the program. The Ramblers haven't played in the NCAA tournament since 1985's Sweet 16 team.

"We don't feel like (the final) is going to be the last game for us or the game after that," said forward Donte Ingram, who scored eight points with a team-high eight rebounds. "If we do what we need to do, we can play and beat anybody."

Loyola (27-5) has won nine straight games since losing Jan. 31 at Bradley. Up next is their first conference tournament title game since 2002, when they played in the Horizon League.

The fifth-seeded Braves (20-13), who trailed by 14 points near the end of the first half, never let up. But Loyola always seemed to answer with a big 3-pointer.

None was as vital as Marques Townes' bomb with 1 minute, 25 seconds left that put the Ramblers ahead 59-54 after neither team had scored for more than three minutes with Loyola clinging to a two-point lead.

"I just had an open look," said Townes, who scored 12 points. "It felt good. I was confident in my shot. I was 0-for-4 last game, but the coaches said just keep shooting."

The Ramblers emerged from the final media timeout holding up four fingers, reminding themselves to lock down defensively for the last few minutes.

The Braves pulled within 54-53 on a layup by Nate Kennell (12 points) with 6:42 to go. Loyola held them to one point after that as Bradley missed its last seven shots from the field.

Ramblers point guard and MVC player of the year Clayton Custer returned to form with 12 points and four assists after he hurt his ankle in the quarterfinal win over Northern Iowa and shot a combined 2-of-17 in the previous two games.

"I love our guys' mentality," Moser said. "They just refused to quit. You look at how many grind-out games we've had, especially the last several weeks. We just find ways to win. Different guys, different nights." ∎

Clayton Custer makes a move and drives on Bradley Braves guard Dwayne Lautier-Ogunleye. Loyola won the MVC Tournament semifinal 62-54, and Custer had 12 points in the win. (AP Images)

LET'S DANCE

'Blessed' Moser Leads Ramblers Back to Tourney for First Time Since 1985

BY SHANNON RYAN

When Porter Moser accepted the head coaching job at Loyola in 2011, he believed it was a good fit for a few reasons. Among them, the potential storybook narrative of a local boy's success.

"I was telling friends and family, 'I'm a Catholic kid from Chicago,'" said Moser, a Naperville native. "'How cool would it be for Loyola to go to the NCAA tournament?' And some of them were looking at me like I was nuts."

Moser, 49, will indeed take the Jesuit school on the lake to its first NCAA appearance since 1985. In his 14th season as a head coach – the last seven with Loyola – he will coach on the largest stage of his career when the Ramblers go dancing.

That was assured with the Ramblers' 65-49 victory against Illinois State in the Missouri Valley Conference championship game.

"I'm blessed to coach this group," Moser said after cutting down nets at the Scottrade Center.

Moser has steadily built Loyola into a winner with local recruiting. When he took over, only one player from the state was on the roster. Today there are six, including Donte Ingram, the MVC tournament's most

outstanding player. Moser also had to contend with the school's switch from the Horizon League to the Missouri Valley five years ago – and the notion among some critics that the Ramblers didn't belong.

The Ramblers had posted only one 20-win season in their last 26 when he took over. They had struggled through three losing seasons in the previous four. And the NCAA tournament seemed like a pipe dream.

But this wasn't Moser's first rebuild.

And if it appeared easy, let him tell you, it wasn't.

"That rebuild is tough," he said.

Arkansas-Little Rock had gone 4-24 when he was hired for his first head coaching job in 2000. The Trojans recorded three straight 18-win seasons after he took over.

When he left for Illinois State in 2003, the Redbirds were 8-21 the previous season. The program went through three athletic directors in his four seasons before he was fired with a 51-67 record.

He credits the patience he was given at Loyola, which won only seven games in his first season and now enters the tournament with a 28-5 record.

"Any time you invest so much and you don't have easy sailing – and I haven't – it makes it so rewarding

Loyola raises the championship trophy of the Missouri Valley Conference Tournament, where they clinched their first NCAA Tournament berth since 1985. (AP Images)

to sit with a group like this and to be in a league like this and to win it," he said.

Moser, who played at Creighton, became just the second person to win a Missouri Valley Conference tournament championship as both a player and coach, joining Southern Illinois' Chris Lowery.

Without hesitating, he said the achievement is more enjoyable as a player. A few of his teammates from Creighton were in the stands in St. Louis, and Moser talked about the lifelong bond that teammates form.

But he's enjoying this one too.

"I'm so excited for where we're going, where the program's going," he said. "But if you really ask me why I'm excited, it's because (of) the group in the locker room and just the moments we're sharing right now. It's been special." ∎

NCAA TOURNAMENT

John J. Kim/Chicago Tribune

WHY NOT LOYOLA?

The Ramblers Have the Right Mix to Make a Final Four Run

By David Haugh

Every March, a national college basketball audience discovers a local secret and tells a friend in the name of celebrating something good.

Everybody knows about the Dukes and Kentuckys, the North Carolinas and Michigan States, but would as many people know where to find Valparaiso or Dunk City on the sport's map without the NCAA tournament? Or that Middle Tennessee or Northern Iowa are more than just geographic estimations? And how to pronounce Pittsnogle or appreciate a trusty Butler?

Over the years, to the delight of millions, much of America annually adopts an unheralded team that captures our imagination, defies long odds and makes memories that last long after the music to "One Shining Moment" ends.

Why not Loyola in 2018?

Why not consider the possibility of Illinois' only college basketball program to win the NCAA tournament advancing a couple of rounds in this one? Get to know everything about coach Porter Moser's team, from the backcourt brotherhood of Blue Valley Northwest High School graduates Clayton Custer and Ben Richardson, who have played together since third grade in Overland Park, Kan., to Sister Jean Schmidt, the Jesuit school's charming 98-year-old chaplain. Learn as much as possible about honorable Loyola legend Jerry Harkness and the historically significant 1963 national championship team

Loyola Ramblers guard Bruno Skokna rests his hand on the Missouri Valley Conference championship trophy after the team was selected to play in the NCAA Tournament. (Armando L. Sanchez/Chicago Tribune)

that shook society by starting four black players in the "Game of Change."

Start with breaking down the first-round game, 11th-seeded Loyola against a beatable Miami team in Dallas.

Maybe this is the year Cinderella parks her carriage at the L stop in Rogers Park and rambles longer than expected. Maybe Loyola can bust its share of brackets the way other double-digit seeds have in recent memory, from No. 15 Florida Gulf Coast soaring into the Sweet 16 in 2013 to No. 11s George Mason and Virginia Commonwealth going to the Final Four in 2006 and 2011, respectively. Those who scoff at the suggestion forget how 13th-seeded Bradley made the Missouri Valley Conference proud in 2006 with a Sweet 16 appearance and another Loyola – 11th-seeded Loyola Marymount – inspired everyone 28 years ago with a run to the Elite Eight after the sudden on-court death of star Hank Gathers.

More than the rest, this is the month sports fans believe in magic, three weeks of suspending reality for fantasy, a time to tap into your Dick Vitale and let emotions spill about absolutely everything from Diaper Dandies to PTPers. This is a short period of time to simply accept that a tournament that produced $761 million in 2017 provides experiences money can't buy. Like it or not, as the FBI continues to investigate college basketball, the court of public opinion still figures to adjourn in April after finding sport's greatest tournament a repeat offender, guilty of stealing the country's attention.

The Ramblers represent the best things about the sport, a model mid-major Division I program balancing academics and athletics in a culture defined by character and integrity, the way Northwestern did a year ago in breaking its 78-year drought. It was after seeing Northwestern break new ground that Loyola players – well aware that their program had gone 32 years without an NCAA bid – started asking themselves: "Why not us?"

The increased exposure never got in the way of execution for the Wildcats, who took advantage of their tournament opportunity by beating Vanderbilt and giving Gonzaga all it could handle. Likewise, expect Loyola to arrive in Dallas ready for its close-up.

Everything starts with Moser, the disciple of Rick Majerus, whose meticulousness can be seen in the way Loyola plays defense and spreads the floor on offense. Moser represents the example every struggling college coach wants his athletic director to notice, a guy whose first Loyola team went 7-23 – and struggled through two more losing seasons before a shift in direction coincided with a move to the MVC. Loyola stuck with Moser – "Just a Catholic kid from Chicago," he says – and success followed.

Along the way came smart, skilled players Moser recruited from winning high school programs.

Custer, the Iowa State transfer who was named MVC player of the year, has more answers than Siri in directing Loyola's offense. Richardson, the conference defensive player of the year, happily does the dirty work. Donte Ingram, the pride of Simeon and most valuable player of the MVC tournament, offers athleticism and leadership the Ramblers lean on through the toughest of times.

Cameron Krutwig, the 6-foot-9 center from Jacobs High in Algonquin who was MVC freshman of the year, prepared for this season by losing 35 pounds and became a passer skilled enough for the offense to go through him at the high post. Marques Townes, a New Jersey high school teammate of NBA star Karl-Anthony Towns, has made a name for himself by shooting 40 percent from behind the 3-point arc. Aundre Jackson, a junior-college transfer, is just as deadly from long range. Lucas Williamson, the freshman from Young who followed Ingram's path from the Chicago Public League, showed uncommon maturity coming through in the clutch in St. Louis.

Five Ramblers average in double figures, led by Custer at 13.4 per game. Moser trusts every last one of them to play an important role, big or small, for a team that makes basketball fun to watch.

An analytics website called Synergy Sports gave Loyola an 11 percent chance of reaching the Sweet 16, according to the Washington Post.

The head says that still sounds a little high. The heart says just shut up and enjoy the ride on a bandwagon filling up fast. ■

Marques Townes, center, celebrates with teammates at a Selection Sunday watch party at Gentile Arena in Chicago. (Armando L. Sanchez/Chicago Tribune)

MARCH 15, 2018 · DALLAS, TEXAS

LOYOLA 64, MIAMI 62

SWISH COME TRUE

Ingram's shot is everything people love about Loyola

BY DAVID HAUGH

Loyola calls the play "Attack," fitting for the tenacious team that captured America's imagination with a pulsating, buzzer-beating 64-62 victory over Miami in the first round of the NCAA tournament.

When Miami guard Lonnie Walker IV missed a free throw with 9.3 seconds left at the American Airlines Center and Loyola guard Ben Richardson came down with the rebound, players knew what to run because they practice such things. At Loyola, they rehearse success.

Had center Cameron Krutwig rebounded the ball, coach Porter Moser would have called a timeout, but a guard grabbing the board provided the cue to push the ball upcourt. So Richardson passed to guard Marques Townes, who quickly dribbled down the floor as teammate Donte Ingram yelled from behind, "Marques, Marques!"

"I heard him loud and clear," Townes said. "They were all on me. I just gave it to Donte."

The pass came with 2.5 seconds left to Ingram, who, naturally, stood just inside the blue March Madness logo about 30 feet from the basket. Ingram, who had missed 5 of 7 3-pointers to that point, never hesitated. He squared up and buried a beautiful left-handed jumper for one of the biggest shots in Dallas since the days of J.R. Ewing.

The buzzer went off. Bedlam ensued. Adrenaline carried Ingram toward the raucous Ramblers cheering section, where he looked for his parents, Don and Doretha. They had traveled from Chicago to see their son's Bryce Drew moment, assuring him a spot in this year's "One Shining Moment."

A replay review showed Ingram's shot went in with 0.3 seconds left, but it already had been etched indelibly into our collective NCAA memories as a gut-wrenching, heart-stopping game-winner.

"Any one of us could have hit that shot, but I was just fortunate enough to be in the position," Ingram said. "I like to think I've got limitless range."

Suddenly, the same word applies to Loyola's potential, with Tennessee standing between the Ramblers and a Sweet 16 appearance. By the time Ingram showered, he was appearing on more highlight shows than Ernie Johnson and trending on Twitter, where former President Barack Obama congratulated the Ramblers and Sister Jean Dolores Schmidt, the team's adorable 98-year-old chaplain.

By the time Ingram is as old as Loyola legend Alfredrick Hughes, the 1985 star who watched from behind the bench in a gold shirt and matching 10-gallon hat, he will savor reliving his heroics at every reunion.

The Loyola bench is ecstatic following Donte Ingram's game-winning 3-point basket against No. 6 seed Miami. (John J. Kim/Chicago Tribune)

"Even when we were down seven, it was just about keep fighting ... We're in the huddle, and it wasn't any panic." – Porter Moser

"What an unbelievable shot for a kid to hit in the NCAA tournament to win it," Moser said. "How many shots in the backyard do you say that to yourself? Those are the things you dream about."

The reality is everything about the play that made Ingram a March icon epitomized Loyola basketball: execution, communication and aggressiveness. Moser also saw significance in the pass from Townes to Ingram becoming Loyola's 19th assist on 26 field goals – the eye-opening statistic Miami coach Jim Larranaga cited as the game's most important.

"Quintessential unselfishness," Moser said.

Nobody embodied that notion more than Richardson, who influenced the outcome without scoring a point. He had five rebounds, one block, one steal and eight assists – perhaps the biggest when he found Clayton Custer for a corner 3 that tied the score at 60 with 1 minute, 16 seconds left.

"That's another example of Ben knowing where I'm going to be before anybody else," Custer said of his longtime friend from Kansas.

Added Moser: "Ben was unbelievable. The kid does anything he needs to do to win."

Finding a way to survive this one and advance revealed the resilience of a Loyola team that has lost just once in 19 games since Jan. 7. After both teams finished a ragged first half tied at 28, it was as if Miami realized Loyola couldn't hang with the Hurricanes above the rim. The emphasis on attacking Loyola's interior created a 43-36 Miami lead that reminded the Ramblers they weren't in the Missouri Valley Conference anymore.

"Even when we were down seven, it was just about keep fighting," Moser said. "We're in the huddle, and it wasn't any panic."

Every possession mattered in the final 10 minutes. Every defensive stop, from Krutwig's steal with 2:12 left to Lucas Williamson's with 23 seconds left, felt like the decisive one. Players drew energy from a Loyola crowd that rocked the building as if it sat in Rogers Park.

"L-U-C!" they chanted after big plays. The Loyola band constituted a larger contingent than the Miami cheering section. Enough people wore maroon-and-gold scarves to make other teams' fans wonder if they had stumbled into a Harry Potter fan convention.

"Loyola Nation was unbelievable," said Moser, who even complimented the team's police escort.

As the kinetic coach conducted a postgame interview on the court, a group of young rowdies reached the railing before a security guard stopped them from going farther.

"We love you, Porter!" they shouted.

Moser just smiled but not any wider than Sister Jean. Minutes after the game, a Loyola employee wheeled the revered nun onto the floor. As every player approached the Ramblers' biggest fan, she made a thumbs-up sign. Talk about a sister act; the sweet scene reinforced why this likable Loyola team connects with so many people.

"You brought the magic today," Richardson told Sister Jean.

Ingram gently hugged her. So did Custer, the last player to head into a giddy locker room.

"Her prayers definitely mean a little bit extra," Custer said. "She's a huge part of our success."

And the spunky 11th-seeded team from Chicago that believes in March miracles said, "Amen." ∎

Loyola guard Donte Ingram hit his crucial 3-point shot with 0.3 seconds remaining to send the Ramblers to the NCAA Tournament second round. (John J. Kim/Chicago Tribune)

NCAA TOURNAMENT SECOND ROUND
MARCH 17, 2018 · DALLAS, TEXAS
LOYOLA 63, TENNESSEE 62

ROCKY TOPPLED

With Help From Merciful Bounce, Custer Lifts Loyola to Sweet 16

By David Haugh

Extending both arms as wide as they would go, Loyola coach Porter Moser faced his adoring fans at the American Airlines Center and broke into a smile that really did seem bigger in Texas.

"I love you guys!" Moser shouted.

Moser applauded the crowd and reached over a railing to join hands with his wife, Megan. He hugged Sister Jean Dolores Schmidt, the 98-year-old team chaplain whose prayers were answered in Loyola's last-second 63-62 NCAA tournament thriller over Tennessee. He looked up into the cheering section full of maroon and gold scarves and T-shirts, soaking in the school's first Sweet 16 appearance in 33 years.

"I don't want to leave," Moser said to nobody in particular.

Now he doesn't have to.

With 3.6 seconds left, guard Clayton Custer got the luckiest bounce of his basketball career when his 15-foot jumper from the right side near the free-throw line fell through the net and Tennessee players dropped their heads. Rocky toppled.

Two days earlier, against Miami, teammate Donte Ingram etched his name into NCAA lore with a buzzer-beating 3-pointer, and this was Custer's turn to play hero.

Down 62-61 with 11 seconds left, Custer left the timeout determined this would not be his last stand. The play called for Custer, the Missouri Valley Conference player of the year, to receive a ball screen from Cameron Krutwig and create something dribbling to the right against Tennessee guard Jordan Bone. Hearing Custer describe the plan at the postgame podium, Moser interrupted his star.

"We still got another game – you can go left," Moser cracked.

Regardless of where Loyola goes for late-game heroics these days, somebody emerges. But as Custer's shot bounced off the front of the rim and off the glass before falling through, it was fair to wonder ever so briefly if the Ramblers were going home.

"I knew it fell kind of short, but I thought it might rattle in," Custer said. "For all that hard work to result in that lucky bounce, the basketball gods helped that one go in."

Perhaps, but as tightly as Sister Jean might have clutched her rosary beads, Loyola prevailed because of precise execution more than divine intervention and players as talented as they are blessed. Every time Tennessee threatened, Loyola thwarted it. When little-used Bruno Skokna buried a 3-pointer for his first points with 10:03 left to give Loyola a 50-41 lead,

Clayton Custer (13) aims for the game-winning basket in the final seconds against Tennessee. Custer made the 2-point jumper with 3.6 seconds remaining to seal Loyola's 63-62 upset. (John J. Kim/Chicago Tribune)

Ramblers fans rose to their feet and a sense of inevitability arrived. This was their night. This is their year, no matter what happens next.

Against a physically superior Tennessee team, Loyola focused on everything that makes its offense fun to watch and hard to guard: ball movement, shot fakes and blockouts. If it wasn't Custer's shooting or Ingram's creating, it was Aundre Jackson's maneuvering for a game-high 16 points, Krutwig's keen passing or Ben Richardson doing whatever Moser asked.

"We talked about not settling, shot-faking, going downhill, and that fits into what we have been doing all year," Moser said.

An out-of-bounds alley-oop to Ingram out of a timeout with 6:47 left reminded everyone why coachable teams are so capable of upsets every March.

This was a statement about the beauty of basketball when executed by smart and selfless players following a detailed plan, a nod for aesthetics over athleticism, a victory for the middle guy. This was another mid-major step forward for college basketball, an instructional video Loyola turned into a highlight reel. This was teamwork at its finest and NCAA sports at their best. This was L-U-C-ing is believing for the top program in Chicago and Illinois.

A reporter asked Loyola players about winning despite being "not the most imposing-looking team."

Richardson interjected.

"We're not scary looking?" he kidded.

Miami and Tennessee would argue otherwise, but the point about Loyola resembling a team you might see in a sequel to *Hoosiers* underscored how much Moser did more with less this weekend. And it's something the rah-rah coach used to his advantage before the biggest game of his players' lives.

"Coach was preaching it's not the size of the dog in the fight, it's the size of the fight in the dog, and I know that's cliché but that's something we've really embraced," Richardson said.

The Ramblers relied on that resolve to pull through a shaky start. Salute Tennessee's Admiral Schofield for that. The Zion-Benton product showed no interest in adding another chapter to the feel-good story back in his hometown, scoring three 3-pointers and a breakaway dunk in the first 4:23 to give the Vols a 15-6 lead.

"I think he said, 'I'm an Illinois guy, I'm going to give it to them right out of the gate,'" Moser said. "Wow, he was hot. We had to regroup."

During a timeout, Moser reamed his players as badly as he had in a month. The tough love worked.

"You can get on kids if they know you love them," Moser said.

Added Krutwig: "He just said, 'This isn't us. This isn't the way to go out,' and our mindset changed."

Over the final 35 minutes, Loyola outscored Tennessee by 10 and Schofield scored only three more points. The Vols played without injured starter Kyle Alexander, and Schofield ran into foul trouble, but nothing can diminish what Loyola accomplished. Give Maryland-Baltimore County its due for becoming the first No. 16 seed to win an NCAA tournament game, ousting top-seeded Virginia, but Loyola deserves all the national attention coming its way.

Moser looked forward more to the local reaction.

"I can't imagine St. Paddy's Day in Chicago," Moser said, laughing. "Wow, my younger self would have loved to have been there."

Moser's older self is having the time of his life in the middle of the madness, with no plans to leave anytime soon. ∎

Guard Lucas Williamson (1) and forward Christian Negron (12) celebrate earning a spot in the Sweet 16. (John J. Kim/Chicago Tribune)

LOYOLA BASKS IN THE HOOPLA

Ramblers Won't Say It, But Are on Brink of 'Basketball Immortality'

BY DAVID HAUGH

For a brief moment, Loyola coach Porter Moser permitted his mind to wander to a place he has marked off-limits for his players' thoughts.

"We haven't sat there and said, 'You guys, this is for the Final Four!' which sounds crazy, doesn't it?" Moser said outside the Loyola locker room. "I mean, it sounds really cool. But I haven't said that to the guys."

Moser doesn't have to. They know. After three straight nail-biting victories in March that have turned Loyola into America's team, almost everybody knows the stakes when the Ramblers tip off against Kansas State at Philips Arena in the NCAA tournament South Region final.

Heck, they unveiled a bobblehead Friday of Sister Jean Dolores Schmidt, Loyola's lovable 98-year-old team chaplain. Maroon-and-gold scarves haven't been this trendy to wear since the days of Gryffindor, and Clayton Custer's popularity probably rivals Harry Potter's. In Chicago, where the Bulls stunk and the Blackhawks slid, Loyola saved a sports winter from complete discontent by supplying the most entertaining, unlikely local college season since Northwestern

went to the 1996 Rose Bowl.

Just don't suggest to Moser that his team has played so well under pressure lately to give the Ramblers an edge over Kansas State in the first NCAA tournament game ever between No. 11 and No. 9 seeds.

"Oh, we're the underdog," Moser said, correcting his questioner. "We're chasing."

Bruce Weber's edgy Wildcats can be caught, but it won't be easy. They ousted Kentucky on Thursday and plan to carry that confidence onto the court against Loyola seeking Kansas State's first Final Four since 1964, when famed former Bulls assistant Tex Winter was coach. Weber, who spent nine seasons at Illinois after a successful stint at Southern Illinois, traditionally builds programs guided by the same principles Moser espouses, which means these are two coaches who never will be on a first-name basis with an NCAA enforcement official or FBI investigator. If KenPom ranked integrity, Weber and Moser would be near the top every year.

Weber has enjoyed better consistency than popularity in six seasons at Kansas State but expressed more pride than vindication when asked about

Nevada forward Cody Martin (11) defends Marques Townes (5) in the second half of Loyola's 69-68 Sweet 16 win. (John J. Kim/Chicago Tribune)

criticism he has received for prioritizing high-level character over five-star talent.

"I used to listen to talk radio and then I became a head coach and I had to go to country music just to have something to listen to and not hear people talk about me," said Weber, 62. "I just tried to do it right, the way I feel it should be done. I don't like what is going on in our business, to be honest. But all I can worry about is myself and making sure that I do things the right way. I know when the paper comes to your door or the news comes on, my kids don't have to worry that I did something I'm not supposed to."

The last time Weber and Moser coached against each other, the biggest loser was a chair. Weber smashed it during a halftime tirade Jan. 4, 2004, when Moser's Illinois State team gave his Illini all they could handle at Assembly Hall. Both were in the middle of their first seasons with their respective teams.

"It sticks in my craw, that game," Moser recalled. "I remember it vividly."

Illinois beat Illinois State 80-73 but needed overtime and a heroic effort from sophomore Deron Williams, who scored 20 points with his jaw wired shut. Moser's Redbirds blew a nine-point lead in the final five minutes.

"We had to play our butts off," Weber said.

From SIU to Illinois to Kansas State, Weber's teams always do. No matter the school colors, the blue-collar emphasis never changes. Weber finds ways to get through to players, often relying on the advice of Oak Brook-based life coach Jim Fannin – with whom he consulted to get Kansas State in the right mindset.

"I have a ton of respect for what Bruce has done at every stop of his journey," Moser said.

So does Loyola guard Donte Ingram, who spent his childhood in Danville, Ill., about 30 miles from Champaign rooting for Weber's Illini.

"I was a big fan of Dee Brown and all those guys, and that was a big thing when they were going up

Assistant coach Bryan Mullins, left, and head coach Porter Moser, right, offer instruction and encouragement to Loyola players. (John J. Kim/ChicagoTribune)

against North Carolina on their great run," Ingram said. "Another guy from the 217 (area code)."

The guy from the 217 knows from experience Moser will have the men from the 773 mentally prepared for anything and everything.

"I know because of Tony Barone, because of Coach Rick Majerus, guys that (Moser) had gone through, he has a little bit of both those guys, the toughness, the defense, the scheming, the discipline, the shot fakes, all those stuff I watched those coaches do," Weber said of Moser. "And he does it, and that's why they're good. He's a good guy for the business, and I'm happy he got a second chance."

Moser's surprise firing at Illinois State in 2007 sent him on a serendipitous path to Saint Louis under Majerus and eventually home to Chicago where, seven years after taking the Loyola job, he is 40 minutes away from being the hottest coach in the country.

Nowadays, people listen when Moser questions a flawed NCAA selection committee process that would have left Loyola out of the 68-team field if the Ramblers had stumbled in the MVC tournament. They ask about the detailed notes he hangs in the locker room pregame and his thoughts on the motion offense.

They smile as he relives a White House visit five years ago with the 1963 Loyola national champions to honor "The Game of Change," that broke racial barriers.

They enjoy everything about a Loyola story that stands an excellent chance of getting even better as the tournament progresses.

"I love how our team has been embraced because I think we play the right way," Moser said.

Anybody know the way to San Antonio?

"We just want to win the next game," Loyola senior Ben Richardson said. "We're not necessarily thinking about basketball immortality."

But that's what awaits Loyola with one more victory, an exciting possibility not even its coach could suppress. ∎

The Loyola Ramblers stand together for the national anthem before facing No. 7 seed Nevada in the Sweet 16. (John J. Kim/Chicago Tribune)

NCAA TOURNAMENT ELITE EIGHT

MARCH 24, 2018 · ATLANTA, GEORGIA

LOYOLA 78, KANSAS STATE 62

'WE'RE NOT DONE'

Ramblers Become Just Fourth No. 11 Seed to Reach Final Four

By David Haugh

The coach of the team that lets nothing get in its way climbed across the press table at Philips Arena and made his way into the third row of rowdiness.

Porter Moser hugged his wife, Megan, whose eyes were moist, before embracing his crying teenage daughter, Jordan, and each of his sons, Jake, Ben and Max.

Maroon-and-gold mania surrounded the Mosers in the stands and on the floor, the euphoria created by Loyola's emphatic 78-62 victory over Kansas State in the NCAA tournament South Region final that earned the school a trip to the Final Four in San Antonio.

"We did it," Moser said into his wife's ear.

Yes, as inexplicable as it seems, Loyola did it, going to the Final Four for the first time in 55 years and becoming only the fourth No. 11 seed to do so.

Cinderella is off to the Alamo – and it promises to be a trip to remember.

After returning to the court for the celebration, Moser grabbed the microphone as captains Ben Richardson and Donte Ingram hoisted a trophy in front of their teammates, who all wore black "Final Four" hats. Sister Jean Dolores Schmidt, the international celebrity smiling in her wheelchair, accepted hugs from players on their way to the grandest stage of their lives.

"How about them Ramblers?" Moser screamed

like a basketball evangelist. "I want to give glory to God, who has been so good to our Jesuit university ... "

Moser paused, peered around at the adoring Loyola fans and grinned from ear to ear.

"Look at this. Are you kidding me?" Moser shouted. "This is the way it's supposed to be."

This is what it looks like when everything comes together for a college basketball program, when the winning gene and Sister Jean provide the intangibles and talented players do the rest.

Loyola made an Elite Eight matchup in March against Kansas State resemble a conference game in January against Missouri State. Against a Big 12 team known for its defense, Loyola's offense efficiently executed its game plan better than anyone could have hoped in shooting 57.4 percent. Loyola trailed for 38 seconds – when the score was 4-3. The Ramblers smothered Bruce Weber's Kansas State team, which shot 34.8 percent.

"This is the moment you dream about as kids," Ingram said.

Sister Jean's prayers were answered and – OMG – what a beautiful display of basketball it was as Loyola spread the floor and shared the ball in a two-hour, nationally televised clinic on fundamentals.

"We came out really noisy on defense, yelling

Head coach Porter Moser hoists the net after beating Kansas State to advance to the Final Four in San Antonio.
(John J. Kim/Chicago Tribune)

"It's been quite a metamorphosis because the *Loyola Phoenix* was the only one in the press conference for about 20 games. All summer long, we were like, 'Why not us?'" – Porter Moser

out everything," Moser said. "You could just see them getting stops, and I think they knew right away our defense was dictating everything and the confidence was growing."

You will remember where you were when you watched this game, one of the most impressive, improbable Chicago sports achievements in decades. The 2016 Cubs and 1985 Bears always will occupy a special place in the city's history, taking nothing from the Bulls dynasty, the 2005 White Sox or the Blackhawks' run of three Stanley Cups since 2010.

But as far as local college stories go, none since Loyola's 1963 national title surpass this one because nobody saw this resurgence out of Rogers Park coming except, perhaps, the guys on campus.

"It's been quite a metamorphosis because the Loyola Phoenix was the only one in the press conference for about 20 games," Moser kidded postgame when asked a question by a reporter from the campus newspaper. "All summer long, we were like, 'Why not us?'"

But how do you explain it?

You run out of words. You exhaust the supply of adjectives. You look for new ways to describe the indescribable because everything sounds so wonderfully redundant. Everything seems too good to be true, an elite college basketball team made up of a bunch of

With the 78-62 win over Kansas State, Loyola advanced to the Final Four for the first time since 1963.

guys you wanted to live on the same block growing up.

This is how relatable Loyola's players are: Back at the team hotel after the pregame shootaround, someone wanted to take a picture with a group of players. The fan asked Clayton Custer to take it, not realizing the Missouri Valley Conference player of the year was on the team.

"And Clay was so polite he was going to do it without saying anything," best friend Ben Richardson said.

Loyola going to the Final Four represents the best of college basketball, a victory for character, coachability and all that is right about sports, a win for the good guys. The Ramblers didn't do this because of a single superstar or one blue-chip recruiting class. They did it with a whole greater than the sum of its parts, more collectively than individually, by stressing team over me the old-fashioned way.

Everyone sensed it would be Loyola's night when its first five baskets each came from different starter. Center Cameron Krutwig posted up as strong as a fullback and passed like a point guard. Ingram delivered his typical all-around athleticism. Marques Townes never stopped attacking. Custer shot poorly but contributed a team-high five assists on a night his best buddy rose to the occasion.

Richardson, the guy known for doing all the little things, came up biggest when Loyola needed him most. The senior guard reached his season high of 15 points with 14 minutes left and finished with a career-high 23. After Richardson was fouled on a 3-pointer that resulted in a four-point play, he lay flat on his back and extended his arms like a kid making a snow angel. How appropriate that Richardson emerged as the hero after Ingram, Custer and Townes each played the role in the first three NCAA tournament victories.

Big Ben, they can call him on campus now.

The Loyola Ramblers celebrate with the South Regional trophy following their Elite Eight victory, a true team effort for the ages. (John J. Kim/Chicago Tribune)

"I was in a rhythm and they were finding me," Richardson said. "It was the biggest game of my life."

Remember the NCAA selection committee declared that Loyola, the MVC champion by four games, needed to survive its league tournament to make the field of 68. Now the Ramblers are one of the last four teams standing. Somehow, that farce only makes this all the more satisfying for Loyola.

"To see these guys experience that is an amazing feeling as a coach," Moser said.

The atmosphere in the crowd of 15,477 possessed a definite Loyola vibe from the opening tipoff, when familiar chants of "L-U-C!" echoed throughout the arena. Fans and alumni in Gryffindor scarves and Loyola T-shirts showed up in bigger numbers and louder than ever, with the student newspaper, the *Phoenix*, even beefing up its coverage with seven staffers.

Loyola legend Jerry Harkness and teammates from the 1963 national championship team moved their seats to behind the Ramblers bench to watch this history.

Three of Moser's Creighton teammates – Matt Petty of Colorado Springs, Colo.; Todd Eisner, the head coach of Winona State, and Craig Seibert of Omaha, Neb. – flew in to see their friend seize the moment and stood the entire game at their courtside seats.

"This team is blessed," Harkness said with pride as Loyola players cut down the nets.

This team believes it belongs in the Final Four, and confidence is its greatest weapon.

"We're not done," Ingram said.

Why not Loyola? ∎

Guards Clayton Custer (13), Ben Richardson (14) and Donte Ingram (0) motion to the crowd after a basket by Ingram during the second half in Atlanta. (John J. Kim/ Chicago Tribune)

FINAL FOUR'S BRIGHTEST STAR

Sister Jean: 'This Is the Most Fun I've Had in My Life'

BY SHANNON RYAN

Forty news cameras were trained toward a small stage. Approximately 200 reporters crammed into the room, waiting for the star.

Then a moderator made an announcement, "Sister Jean is in the building."

Sister Jean Dolores Schmidt was wheeled in, up a ramp and – naturally – onto center stage.

"Ready to roll?" moderator Mark Fratto asked her.

"You better believe it," Sister Jean replied.

The 98-year-old Loyola team chaplain was the celebrity of Friday's Final Four media news conferences. Actually, who are we kidding? She's the celebrity of the tournament.

"I walked by, I thought it looked like Tom Brady at the Super Bowl," Loyola coach Porter Moser said.

Reporters who have covered the NCAA tournament for decades and NCAA officials could not recall a breakout-room session with more media. With a gold-and-maroon scarf draped around her neck and wearing a black Loyola shirt with her letterman's jacket on her lap, Sister Jean marveled at the attention.

Sister Jean Dolores Schmidt receives a hug from Clayton Custer following Loyola's win over Tennessee in the NCAA tournament. Custer's basket with 3.6 seconds remaining sealed the 63-62 win to advance to the Sweet 16. (John J. Kim/Chicago Tribune)

"I'm amazed at what the different channels and radio stations and all the reporters from all the papers and so forth do," she said. "I think to myself, 'Oh my, don't let it go to your head.' I haven't done that, nor has the team."

In the midst of the hoopla, Sister Jean offered thoughts on praying ("I always ask God to be sure that the scoreboard indicates the Ramblers have the big 'W'"), mottos for life ("Worship, Work and Win") and whether God is a basketball fan ("He's probably a basketball fan more of the NCAA than the NBA").

Witty as usual, she said about her best-selling bobblehead (the third version ever made of her), "I think the company could retire when they're finished making these bobbleheads."

Moser later joked about his original autographed Sister Jean bobblehead, "I might be a pseudo name on eBay putting it out there."

Loyola players were tickled about the nun they've loved for years receiving this recognition. They joked about how much more packed her media session was than theirs but appreciate that Sister Jean's positive messages are being broadcasts around the globe.

"We all think it's awesome," Clayton Custer. "We laugh about it too. It's really cool. We've all known about her for so long. We've known how special she is. It's cool that everybody in the world knows who she is now and they're getting to see how cool she is and how amazing she is really."

Sister Jean was fitting in time for Mass on Good Friday and also planned for Easter Sunday in San Antonio. Yes, she said, she plans for the Ramblers to beat Michigan on Saturday and still be in Texas, playing for the national championship on Monday.

Loyola's sports information staff purposefully planned one media session during the Final Four in hopes of cutting down on the overwhelming demand.

For her part, she's having a blast.

"This is the most fun I've had in my life," she said.

And what a life she's had.

She left reporters with one last gem before being wheeled out of the room.

"You're great people," she said. "Don't let anyone put you down." ■

Sister Jean Dolores Schmidt prays with the Ramblers players before Loyola's Elite Eight matchup against Kansas State in Atlanta. (John J. Kim/Chicago Tribune)

CHEERS AMID TEARS

Run Ends as Michigan Takes Over in 2nd Half

By David Haugh

On their last trip off the basketball court together as teammates Saturday night, Loyola guards Clayton Custer and Ben Richardson, best friends since third grade, walked with arms around one another down an Alamodome tunnel as they fought back tears.

Richardson pulled his maroon No. 14 jersey over his red face as Custer hugged his buddy a little tighter, both trying to process the disappointment of a 69-57 loss to Michigan in the NCAA tournament semifinal.

Eventually their pain will go away. The memories will last forever.

"I think a lot of people will remember this run for a long time," Richardson said at his locker. "I have no regrets."

Nobody at Loyola should, not after one of the more remarkable NCAA tournament runs in decades – and certainly a feel-good story that saved the Chicago sports winter. The Ramblers simply ran into a bigger, better Michigan team that capitalized on their mistakes in a second half when the script for the fairy tale began to stray from its happy ending. Cinderella met Michigan's Moe Wagner, and it ruined her night.

"I know we impacted a lot of lives in our city and across the country but right now that's hard to let sink in," Custer said.

Each Rambler still hugged Sister Jean Dolores Schmidt, the team's 98-year-old celebrity chaplain, before leaving the floor. But this time, the nun consoled the players after her prayers went unanswered. Hail, Michigan prevailed over so many Hail Marys.

When coach Porter Moser gathered his team in the locker room, as tough of a postgame scene as Moser ever has experienced in 28 years of coaching, he spoke from his broken heart.

"When I walked off the floor, I was asked what I said to them and I said, 'The more you invest in something the harder it is to give up,' and they didn't want it to end," Moser said. "I could not be more proud of a group than I am of this group."

Loyola, 32-6, made college basketball relevant again in the city. The Ramblers finished with the winningest season in program history, which included a 14-game winning streak. Seniors Richardson and Donte Ingram won 90 games over their careers, which Moser says went by in a blink.

"I remember moving them in as freshmen, two high-energy, fun young little guys – it just goes so

Guard Marques Townes drives to the basket during the first half of Loyola's Final Four game against Michigan. Townes scored eight points in the first half as Loyola built a 29-22 halftime lead. (Brian Cassella/Chicago Tribune)

fast," Moser said. "To do what they did ... and to do it the right way, the way they are off the court. Not even a littering violation with these guys. What they did was very hard to do."

What the Ramblers couldn't do against Michigan was finish what they started.

The simple answer is Wagner happened. The Moe stands for momentum, which swung in the second half when the German star took over the game. Inside and outside, the 6-foot-11 Wagner dominated, scoring 24 points and grabbing 15 rebounds – nine off the offensive glass. Wagner posted a double-double in the first half. His 3-pointer with 6 minutes, 56 seconds left tied the game 47-47. Loyola's nimble big man, Cameron Krutwig, countered with a team-high 17 points that bode well for the future, but Wagner presented too many problems.

"I liked a lot of things we were doing defensively on him," Moser said. "What happened was he got some offensive rebounds and that was some of the things you give up with our size and he got down on the block."

Michigan shot 57 percent in the second half. It helped that the Wolverines scored 22 points off 17 Loyola turnovers – including five straight during the most damaging second-half stretch. Michigan coach John Beilein's stingiest defensive team in 11 years responded to the urgency of a 10-point deficit and grew more active, forcing Loyola into tougher shots and shorter possessions. Loyola loves the 3-point shot but hit only 1 of 10 attempts. The Wolverines finished the game with a 38-16 spurt.

"It was a painful run, but you have to credit Michigan, they were really shrinking the gap," Moser said. "I don't think it was any one thing. Their length, they're really good defensively. They close the gap of opportunity really fast."

The opportunity seemed there for Loyola's taking after the first 20 minutes.

Loyola coach Porter Moser hugs guard Marques Townes in the final seconds of Loyola's loss to Michigan in the Final Four. (Brian Cassella/Chicago Tribune)

In typical tournament fashion, Loyola fell behind 12-4 with 12:38 left in the first half. The Ramblers got good looks but had bad aim, starting the game only 2 of 10. Michigan struggled too and, at one point, both teams had as many turnovers as field goals. The Ramblers went more than 5– minutes without scoring and 7:39 without making a field goal.

Resilient as ever, Loyola outscored Michigan 25-10 over the final 12 minutes of the half. A 9-0 run restored confidence and reinvigorated the Ramblers with the help of Marques Townes, their best player in the first half whose second-half injury limited Loyola. When Ingram beat the buzzer – sound familiar? – Loyola players pranced into the locker room leading 29-22 and believing they could win this thing.

A sea of maroon and gold in the Loyola section, full of alumni who came from all over the country and hundreds of students who bused 25 hours from Rogers Park, sensed something special in the air. They chanted "L-U-C!" and held up homemade signs such as "We Want The Fairytale," and "We're On A Mission From God." They wore Sister Jean T-shirts – "Worship. Work. Win" – and those familiar Harry Potter-esque scarves. They wanted to extend this Loyola-palooza another 48 hours, but this was Michigan's night to party.

Gracious to the end, Moser congratulated Michigan but spent the bulk of the postgame putting into perspective all his team had accomplished. He smiled wistfully at his players on the podium.

"There's a ton of love in this locker room and it's very hard to end it but there's no end," Moser said. "Like I told these guys, we're going to be connected for life."

In an NCAA tournament that had a once-in-a-lifetime feel, Loyola lost a game but won America's respect. ∎

Guard Clayton Custer puts his head in his hands during Loyola's loss to Michigan in San Antonio. (John J. Kim/ Chicago Tribune)

Armando L. Sanchez/Chicago Tribune